Also by Bruce McCully:

. . . .

Plagued: *The CEO's Ultimate Guide*
to HIPAA Compliance and Cybersecurity

Plagued: *HIPAA and Healthcare*
Cybersecurity Companion Workbook

Accountants: *Your 7 Biggest*
Cybersecurity Mistakes

Space Cow Publishing
Nashville, TN

ISBN: 9798517385734

Book design by Julie Hill

Printed in the United States of America

LEVEL UP

**The Ultimate MSP Road Map for
Improving Security, Operations, and Profitability**

Bruce McCully, CISSP

To the Guardians

A thank you to those working tirelessly
to create safe passage for all who dare
journey through cyberspace.

CONTENTS

Applications

Data

PREFACE

Have you ever worried, as a leader in an MSP, that you are not doing enough to protect your clients?

After spending countless hours talking to other MSP owners and lead engineers, and with more than twenty years' experience running an MSP of my own, I've come to realize that managed service providers are often dealt a bad hand.

When clients are upset because they have a data breach or ransomware event, who are they going to point to first? Who will they want to both deal with the problem and hold responsible for it?

You got it.

And when your team has to figure out evolving technology —especially in the realm of cybersecurity—who is expected to vet, test, and troubleshoot solutions?

Definitely not the vendors of that technology!

The unfortunate truth is that you—the engineer or MSP owner—work where the rubber meets the road. You have to pick up the pieces when things fall apart, whether because of faulty products, implementation headaches, or poor vendor support.

Let's consider your perimeter, for example. I spoke to one MSP owner who considered firewalls a hot topic. He knew his company did not have a good, advanced firewall. He and his team began evaluating the options. They spent hours reading about Fortinet, WatchGuard, and SonicWall, among other solutions. They ended up not having a clue which one to implement.

One day, he went to his team and said, "All right, guys, just pick one." So the team picked the firewall they liked most—not the one that might have been ideally suited for their clients. What this MSP owner really wanted his team to do was pick the best firewall—he wanted them to beat the crap out of it. Kick the tires and really understand what it could handle. Unfortunately, it all boiled down to one thing: they chose the vendor with the sharpest-looking interface.

I've known other MSPs to choose vendors based on whoever makes the best sales pitch. They end up choosing product B for all the wrong reasons. And then they go ahead and hire a level-three tech who has product B experience—blindly making hiring and product decisions just because the vendor's sales team happened to be on the ball that day.

Does this sound at all familiar?

I can tell you that when I was running my own MSP, after I delegated much of the vendor decisions to the VP or operations manager, I always worried that they were making emotionally driven decisions when it came to choosing vendors. There were times when we didn't have the level of knowledge or the time to fully evaluate what our vendors were doing and whether they were doing what they claimed to be doing.

Another problem came up quite frequently. Everybody and his brother was using our stack. We couldn't differentiate our products easily. Our sales team knew we were selling the same exact thing that a dozen other MSPs in our market were selling and they had little confidence in our ability to win deals. Guess what? That lead to lower sales and slower growth.

Then came the nitty-gritty of deploying all this hardware and software in our client environments. In order to do everything right, we needed a full-time security expert who was able to evaluate product A versus product B. They had to deploy it. Then they had to evaluate it again. How well was it configured? Was it configured the way it's supposed to be? Never have I felt more like I was running in circles.

Then, when the you-know-what hits the fan, your vendor is nowhere to be found. When you finally do hunt them down, the sales person who was so easy to track down when you were purchasing the product tells you something like, "Hmmm, sounds like you didn't configure it right" or "You must have missed our latest update."

Do you feel like when one of your clients gets hacked, you are left holding the bag?

Obviously, this is not good enough: vendors with no responsibility, MSPs taking on all the blame, and no one out there testing and improving cyber security stacks. No one even masking small vendor agnostic suggestions on service offerings. Time for a change.

Before I dive into security operations, I want you to think about one final question: What keeps you up at night?

What kept me up at night was the fear that my team wouldn't be able to handle what hackers threw at them. My solution—one that many MSPs have gravitated toward—was vendor-agnostic security training.

Now, by "training," I don't mean sending one of your level-two techs to watch some videos and take a test to become certified in the latest firewall technology from Vendor-X. What I mean is changing the way you help your team learn. Weekly training that raises awareness and having simple missions your team can discuss and execute. I'm talking about sessions that focus on real life problems that face employees at MSPs. Imagine having your entire team learn how to remove a virus from a machine without giving up administrative credentials.

Of course I understand that there are only so many hours in the day and that your techs might not want to spend their evenings and weekends undergoing training. I get that. I also know that there are all sorts of dense subscription-based webinars and videos on the market. Some of them contain valuable information contributed by white-hat hackers. But no one has the time or patience to sit down and listen to them. When my MSP would pay for these training sessions, not a single tech watched them. They didn't have 120 hours to spare for classwork, even though it was already paid for.

That's exactly why I decided to sell my MSP and start helping other MSPs with their security and operations. That's why I am writing this book—to help MSPs create an environment that will enable everyone to become a little more secure than they were yesterday. Security is a journey, and the MSP community is stuck in the mud at the moment. My goal is to help take the guess work out of security, so you can continue this journey.

A little bit about me.

When I was growing up, my dad was a farmer. We weren't exactly rich, but we got by. My mom was a teacher at a local elementary school, and one year when I was around eight years old, she brought home an Apple IIe computer.

Do you remember that computer? It had a green screen, and it didn't come with much software. In fact, it only came with a book, and if you typed in certain commands, you could get the computer to do things - such as fill the entire screen with the words "Hello, world." I loved that computer.

Do you remember the first time you got a computer to do exactly what you wanted it to? Wasn't it amazing!

One afternoon my mom and dad were out baling hay, and they left me at home with the computer. During the two hours they were gone, I took apart every single piece. There were components all over the dining-room table.

I disassembled the computer because I wanted to understand how it worked. I wanted to understand how you could type in these little letters and numbers and fill the entire screen with something that had nothing to do with what you had typed in. I wanted to learn how it worked—and what better way than tear it apart and look inside? To break it down into its constituent parts?

But when my mom got back and saw what I had done, she was very angry. I mean, can you imagine? We couldn't afford that computer. She borrowed it from the school for the summer, and her son had just torn it apart! She'd have to find a way to replace it. Luckily, I was able to put it back together. I'm not sure I'd be here today if I couldn't. (I think my mom would have killed me, and I would never have built the confidence I needed to engage in cyber.)

Growing up on the farm taught me a couple of important lessons. I learned the value of hard work. I learned that I had a knack for computers. I think the most important lesson I learned was the joy of helping people.

You see, it didn't matter whether it was the next-door neighbor whose house burned down and needed a place to stay or if it was the nine foster children we housed over the years. We always figured out a way to help.

That's how I've built my success—by always figuring out a way to help. In fact, I was able to grow my MSP to $8.5 million in annual sales by finding people who shared this very simple ideal: We Enjoy Helping People. Many of you probably know this story already. What you probably don't know is what happened to me a couple of years prior to selling the company.

You see, as the MSP grew, I never got out of tech work. Specifically, the security work. I know, that's cardinal sin for an entrepreneur, but read on, it worked for me. One morning in the spring of 2018 I received a desperate phone call from one of our clients about a ransomware attack on a hospital. Over 700 of their computers were infected and their IT team was overwhelmed. I put together a disaster recovery team with a couple of forensics folks and we headed out to give a hand. I quickly started a separate company, Healthcurity, that solely focused on healthcare – specifically on hospitals and helping them recover from cyberattacks.

I created a goal. A big, crazy, hairy, exciting, new mission: to help protect a million people by 2023. I wrote a book about health-care cybersecurity called *Plagued*, and in it I focused on issues related to healthcare data protection. I outlined the ways facilities were getting infected with ransomware and used the book to get the word out to the medical industry.

We were on the front lines. We would figure out where the hackers were, then we'd pull them out of the network and build a new network in its place. It was a lot of work, but it made you feel good. You felt great knowing that you got everything back up and running. That you were helping a lot of people all at once.

But this work also sucked, and I'll tell you why: at the end of the day, when you're getting ready to go home and an emergency-room doctor asks how long she'll have to wait before she can view CAT scan results, you have to say it's going to be three or four days before those tools come back online.

This means it will be three or four days before the patient who came in this afternoon can be properly diagnosed. It will be three or four days before the doctor can know whether the patient is suffering from a stroke or whether he'll need to be transported to another facility over 150 miles away which was a risk in itself. It was awful!

I remember one facility that had been ransomed after having a security analysis done just months beforehand. Their IT team was completely exhausted; all their servers and all their computers were infected. We could not find a single workstation that was uninfected. We spent weeks putting everything back together, and I kept thinking: how can we get in front of this? How can we change the story? How can we get ahead of these hackers?

Until I saw firsthand the devastation experienced by health-care facilities as a result of ransomware attacks, I didn't fully realize how damaging technology can be. Seeing that hackers were actually able to jeopardize people's lives, I realized that something had to change.

That's when I started changing my mind-set. Instead of having to experience the pain of ransomware remediations, I searched for a better way. How could I help IT directors and their teams understand that their behaviors, habits, and decisions can lead to life-shattering events?

At first, I looked all over the place for some kind of tool, something that would allow us to predict how a hacker could get into a complex environment. I looked at open-source tools. I looked at commercial tools. And then I did what we would do up on the farm.

When you have a tractor that's sixty years old and a part breaks, you can't just go to the store and buy a new one; you build the part yourself. You get the welder out, and you either fix the one that exists, or you fabricate a new one. And that's exactly what I decided to do.

I built the solution myself.

I decided to build a solution that would allow us to scan a network and identify how hackers were getting in—a solution that went much deeper than a full HIPAA security-risk assessment. And then the story started to change. I had meeting after meeting with people who were thrilled that we were finding holes in the system *before* it was hacked.

At that point, what would you do if you were in my place? You're running an $8 million managed service provider. Things are going really well. You've figured out how to help hospitals. What would be your next step?

Here's what I decided to do.

I decided to focus one hundred percent on one thing: ransomware.

Galactic Advisors has analyzed hundreds of managed service providers just like yours, and I'm going to share some of the things we found within their networks. I'm going to share some of the mistakes they made—some of the mistakes that allowed hackers to get in.

I'm going to tell you how you can avoid becoming the next ransomware horror story. On top of it all, I'm going to give you some options to *increase your bottom line at the same time*.

A couple of things before I get started. This isn't a book about how vulnerable you are or how easy it is to get in, because you already know that. You already know the reality of being hacked and having a ransomware event within your MSP.

The second thing is that the MSPs we evaluated were not trunk slammers. They weren't just working out of the backs of their cars. These folks earned between $1 million and $162 million in revenue. They had their stuff together. They knew what they were doing.

So, in the pages that follow, I'm going to share with you the most important steps you can take to keep your cybersecurity stack in place and operational. I'm going to show you how ransomware attacks happen even though you're spending good money on tools that should be working and on staff members who are logging full-time hours on the job. I'm going to show you how your engineers make it easy for hackers. And finally, I'm going to show you how to get secure and stay that way.

Then I'm going to answer the question that people asked me most often while I was writing this book. They asked, "Bruce, what is the one thing we can do to protect our organizations, even if we do nothing else?"

Read on.

INTRODUCTION

How to Create an Effective, Secure, Money-Making MSP

Take a breath for a minute.

If you're a pro cybersecurity guy or gal, with a lot of letters after your name, I'm glad you're here. This book is for you, even if you use it as a refresher course or a quick reference guide. It's chock-full of the minor "gotchas" that even some of the industry's leading MSPs need to be aware of in order to perform a solid checkup on their security operations. And if you're not a pro cybersecurity expert (at least not yet!), there's nothing to fear. This book is also for you.

I am 100 percent certain that every single MSP can create a cybersecurity stack that will protect its clients, protect its own networks, and contribute to its bottom line. I have immense confidence in your ability to secure your clients, sell your services, and be more effective in doing so for two basic reasons.

First, you know more about your business—how it runs, the products you sell, and the services you deliver—than anyone else. Getting your head wrapped around that is the hard part. Resolving security issues and selling your services are easy by comparison.

Cybersecurity contractors brought in to help organizations with their security postures often spend an inordinate amount of time and effort getting to know how their clients work. What makes them tick. And what is critical to their core products. You've already proved an understanding of your security risks simply by cracking this book open. While you may have work to do in order to achieve your overall business goals, you are leaps and bounds above many who lack the fundamental understanding of their enterprises or the risks associated with managed services today. This is a tremendous advantage that you, my friend, possess.

Second, my own background in building an MSP from scratch tells me that just about anybody can learn what I've learned. Anybody can grasp how to build a successful security-centric MSP capable of making a good profit margin and attaining sizable year-over-year growth (I'm talking double digits).

I got my start just as you did, rolling up my sleeves and figuring out what works and what doesn't:

1. I read up on the problems in our industry.

2. I used my insights, intuition, and common sense.

3. I translated what I saw (i.e., what I knew existed) and what I learned into easily understandable communications for the benefit of my clients.

4. I implemented and tested a cybersecurity stack by following a very simple but strict process aimed at continual improvement.

I've been where many of you have been. I vividly remember the Valley of Death—the gap between $2 million and $5 million in revenue. This is where a lot of folks experience growing pains or have a hard time scaling and moving forward. I've been there with my MSP, and I know the challenges you face.

So why am I not still running that company?

Around 2018, we started focusing on recovering hospitals from ransomware. And what I learned is that no matter what we did, hackers would still get in. Even if we had tools that showed people exactly what was going on and what was going wrong, facilities would still get hacked. Eventually, we learned that security isn't so much about having the right tools or plugging all the holes as it is about a mind-set. It's about an organizational culture.

Since I first put pen to paper for this book, I've received hundreds of success stories from MSP owners, IT operations managers, and IT salespeople who had been desperately looking for something better. They've used my security operations calls—weekly calls in which our membership and their teams review critical security operations issues—and super-sales Friday calls, during which clients' sales and marketing teams learn to use penetration tests to find bigger and better opportunities to increase their top-line revenue without having to add to their teams.

Several of our MSP clients have actually doubled their revenue quarter over quarter using our tools and framework. I have been inspired—and hope you will be inspired—by what they've accomplished, even during what some have called the hardest times of our generation.

I do realize that a large part of your success depends on your motivation. I have everything laid out in this book to get you started. The mechanics are here. But ultimately you have to commit to getting the work done. Ultimately you have to go from your first read of this book to following the steps, implementing the changes within your culture and network environment, improving your sales methods, and effectively communicating with and engaging your clients by means of reports and dialogue they can understand.

Here are some tips to launch you on this mission:

1. Don't be intimidated. There's no magic or fancy Ivy League degree required.

2. Recognize the value and power of what you've built. Compile lists of what you know about each of your products and processes—and rethink the reasons why things are done that way.

3. Keep an updated status chart of your own and your clients' security so that you're prepared for the worst.

4. Get your team to think in terms of security. Most of what I talk about in these chapters boils down to how your cyber stack is laid out. If you don't know where to start, consider allocating resources to this. By all means use the worksheet that helped me secure the public school system in the state of Maine (**GalacticScan.com/Worksheet**) as a model.

5. Avoid perfection paralysis and *do* something! Don't worry about creating the best, most perfect cyber stack out of the gate.

Will you have holes? Certainly. But if you don't start somewhere, you'll never be any safer.

6. Don't go overboard. Many people believe that great cybersecurity conscious MSPs have to first invest in a complete overhaul. They think they need to rearchitect their entire network, stack, and team. That's nonsense. No new flashy tool or expensive executive search is worth the time or money.

Over the course of twelve weeks or so—sometimes even a couple of weeks, depending on how motivated you are—you'll notice dramatic changes. Your business will run more like a well-oiled machine. The more you invest in the gradual improvement of your team and processes, the more quickly your clients will see the difference.

My own clients prove it every day. My friend Zoran had clients who wouldn't invest in even basic security layers, such as antivirus software. After running simple penetration tests using our Galactic tool set and emailing them the results—without even a sit-down meeting—he was able to point out how vulnerable they were and sell them his full stack solution.

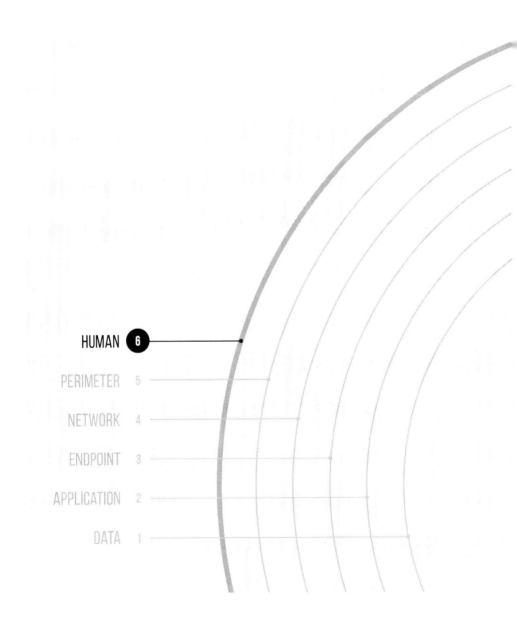

HUMAN **6**

PERIMETER 5

NETWORK 4

ENDPOINT 3

APPLICATION 2

DATA 1

HUMAN

The human layer may be the aspect of your security operation that causes you the most anxiety because you don't have as much control in configuring people as you do in configuring computers!

People don't always work exactly the way you want them to (see chapter 1, "**Why You Need Protection**"). But I'd argue that managing people is no harder—and no easier—than managing any other layer of cybersecurity. They both need the right processes and systems in place in order to be successful.

That's why I'm defining "the human layer" as more than just user activity (see chapter 2, "**Your Cyber Stack**"). I think it also involves how closely you and your team follow instructions (see chapter 3, "**Just-in-Time Documentation**"), how carefully you practice hygiene (see chapter 4, "**Passwords**"), how intelligently you approach risks (see chapter 5, "Cyber Liability Insurance"), how widely you implement policies that fit your core culture (see chapter 6, "**Policies and Procedures**"), and how thoroughly you plan for the inevitable (see chapter 7, "**Tabletop Exercises**").

One of the biggest hurdles here is just getting started.
My advice is simple: start communicating. Start documenting. Start reducing administrative access. Start building your fortress. Just start something.

CHAPTER 1
WHY YOU NEED PROTECTION

You probably have an image of a hacker in your head, right? Somebody sitting around in a sweatshirt working on a computer somewhere.

That's what you probably envision when you think of the word "hacker," and you probably have the idea that this person lives and works in a dorm room or something.

But that's not what we see today when it comes to hackers. We see big businesses staffed by developers focused on one thing and one thing only: deploying and detonating ransomware. This is not a single-hacker situation. There are teams of people who are coordinated and trying to get into your networks.

In fact, one of my biggest fears when I was running an MSP was that I would get a phone call in the middle of the night—somebody calling to tell me that our entire infrastructure was down because one of our user accounts was hacked. That hackers got in and were able to ransom all of our clients at the same time using our remote tools.

When I talk to people about this, I get responses like,
"I'm safe. I don't have to worry about it."

I then ask, "Why do you feel like you're safe?
What do you have in place that makes you feel that way?"

The answers include:

- "I have antivirus software."

- "I have artificial intelligence."

- "I have SIEM."

- "I have backups."

Okay, you get where this is going. But then I often find out later that these people's entire networks were ransomed.

Before I go too much further, let me talk about backups.

When I was growing up, there was this game called Pac-Man. Do you remember?

You're the little Pac-Man. You're the little yellow guy, and you're going around and around, trying to get all the little bits off the board. You're trying to do that before you get caught by the ghosts. Within the first couple of levels of play, the ghosts don't really know where you are. They just bumble around and move all over the board. But as the levels get higher, the ghosts get increasingly interested in where you are, and by the time you reach level 20, as soon as you get on the board, they're headed your way.

If that little yellow guy is your backups, then the ghosts are the ransomware. And the thing about this game is that the little yellow guy never, ever makes it out alive. And in 2021, we're at level 20 when it comes to ransomware. It's pretty sophisticated, and it's pretty good at finding your backups. If your backups are on the same network, as they are in Pac-Man, you will get caught, and your network will be destroyed.

Another thing I hear when I ask people why they feel safe is "I have cloud backups." But that's just another form of Pac-Man. Same game. Just a bigger board. I also hear "I have cloud backups, and they're offline." But I know the numbers. Only half of you who have offline cloud backups have them set up properly. This means that ransomware is able to get to not only your on-site backup but also your cloud backup and your off-site backup.

Yet another thing business owners say is "My IT guy always figures it out." But if you're ransomed, and the ransomware gets to your backups, you're not going to figure it out. The IT guy is not going to figure it out. And guess what? The client knows that the IT guy is you, right? So that's not going to work out for you.

I keep saying that ransomware is getting worse. In 2017, there were $2.3 million in ransomware payments. In 2019, which was also a record year, it jumped to $7.5 *billion*. Think about that. Think about how much money that is. We paid hackers $7.5 billion in 2019.

In 2020, there was a 37 percent increase in ransomware attacks and payments, and 25 percent of those payments resulted from ransomware that was specifically targeted at MSPs.

Now do you understand why hacking is big business and why there are teams of people focused on detonating ransomware inside networks like yours?

The first thing you can do to protect yourself is create a ransomware plan.

Now, we give this a lot of lip service. A lot of people say that they've already created a ransomware plan. If you have, great. But out of the twenty-two MSPs we studied in 2020, only a couple of them had actually written down their plans and communicated them to their teams.

The next thing you can do is practice the plan.

Do you remember when you were in elementary school and you would have a fire drill and an alarm would go off and you would have to leave the school and line up somewhere, maybe by the gymnasium or outdoors on the playground? This was so that everybody would understand what to do in the event of a real fire. That's why they call it a drill. It's not a real fire, but everybody rehearses their emergency procedures.

I'm suggesting you do this at least once per quarter with your own emergency procedures. A key piece of this drill is servicing your clients with your RMM offline. That means you don't have the ability to connect to them remotely. You don't have the ability to log a ticket.

Let me share with you an experience to help you understand where I am coming from and why this so important to me. Often, I am engaged to do a third-party audit or a penetration test depending on the situation. One of the first things we do is an interview. On one occasion, I was interviewing an MSP to learn about how it configured a hospital network. After the interview, I went to meet the owner of the MSP at the facility to do a walk-through and some additional testing.

A brief aside: firewalls are one of the first things we test when it comes to ransomware because they are a last resort protecting your organization. If one of your users clicks a malicious link in an email, you can pretty much guarantee there will be a ransomware payload in the future. First the malicious application will scan the computer, then it will call back to the person who wrote the ransomware for next steps and a ransomware key. If you have a good firewall—that is if you have a smart firewall that's capable of recognizing this type of traffic—it will stop the callback and alert your team. Then you can take care of the problem before any data is exfiltrated, the ransom spreads throughout the organization and often before the computer gets encrypted to begin with. This is really important when it comes to protecting your environments.

So, I'm sitting in one of the hospital's conference rooms. I'm across the table from the owner of the MSP that supports the hospital, and I start my testing. One of the things we do when we test a firewall is actually push a payload that looks a lot like ransomware through it. Usually, the firewall will stop the traffic and alert the SOC, saying, "Hey, there's ransomware coming through," or something along those lines.

But in this case, it went right out, and I pulled another payload back in. I mean, there was nothing even slowing it down. This network was open wide.

I asked, "You know, Mr. MSP Owner, you guys have an advanced firewall installed, right?" That's what we discussed during our interview, and he said, "Of course. Do you want to see it?" I'm thinking that if somebody offers to show me his network room, I am definitely interested. This would be the nerd in me coming out.

We get to the network room, and he opens it up and we start looking around. I'm expecting to see a brand-new advanced firewall capable of IPS / IDS, deep packet inspection, HTTPS proxy, and net flow identification.

There are a couple of things about this type of advanced firewall you should know. First, there's usually a management port. That's how you manage the firewall when the rest of the network is down. Then there are other ports that are used to run the traffic that's going in and out of the network.

We get there, and we look at the rack. The rack is beautiful. Nice wiring job. And at the very top is an old green and white router. This is a ten- to fifteen-year-old router, and there are two of them. You know the type, command line only, great layer 3 router back in the day... but today they belong in a museum. Below them, the brand-new advanced firewalls are sitting in place. But there's something odd going on: there's just one green light lit up on the front, and it's solid. It's not blinking at all. The lights are on, but nobody's home.

So I walk around and look, and there's one purple cable coming out the back of each router. It's just plugged into that management port. That is all. Just the management port.

Whoever set these up went through and installed the firewall. He got it on the management network. He probably even configured it, but he never put it into production. It was just sitting there in the rack, chowing on power. This managed service provider thought it was installed and that it was protecting the hospital environment, but it wasn't doing anything. Heck, they might have even been monitoring it on the management port to make sure it is up, and you bet the hospital was paying for that thing...

And you're probably thinking, "Well, this could never happen to me."

Do me a quick favor, I want you to ask your team. I want you to ask them how they check that a firewall is successfully deployed.

How do you test your IPS and IDS? Do you actually send a payload through to see if it alerts and trace that alert all the way through the SOC to make sure everybody on your team sees it and responds correctly? Or do you just have somebody review the configuration and call it good? You might find out that you don't do any testing at all, when the network is back online, you consider all your work done.

How can you avoid the issue that I ran into? How do you avoid being the MSP who set up a brand-new firewall to find out that it isn't really doing anything?

Yep, that's right, if you don't want to be in that position, you'll have to come up with a way to test your work. You'll have to test your team's work. You'll even have to test your vendors work.

Here's how we do this type of testing for MSPs: we focus on what would happen if an attacker was able to get someone on your team to click a link. The very first thing they are going to do is establish persistence. Create a secondary call back so they can get in if something gets disconnected. Then they'll scan that computer to see what they have immediate access to. So when we're doing analyses for MSPs, we do the same thing. We look at the machine to see what's on it.

Let me share with you some of the results. One day, we were doing an assessment for an MSP, and we came across a few passwords—three passwords, to be exact—on one of its engineers' computers. With those three passwords, which we were able to decrypt, we could figure out the pattern the MSP was using for all its passwords for all its clients. We used the history of that computer and its browser to identify all the external IP addresses that the passwords were used to manage—i.e., this client's cloud infrastructure.

Holy cow! We had found a password treasure trove and gained access to the MSP's entire cloud infrastructure.

I scheduled an emergency call with the CEO of that MSP. Then I sat down with him over a quick video call, and we got started.

Imagine for a minute that you're me and that you're about to tell this guy that you have all the passwords for all his clients and access to his entire cloud infrastructure. I got a little nervous. I don't know why. Maybe I was nervous for him? Anyway I started to describe the situation.

"We need you to change these passwords right away," I said.

Then he said, "We use two-factor authentication. It's okay. It doesn't matter, because we're still safe."

Duh. He has two-factor authentication. Let's dig into what two-factor authentication just so we're all on the same page. Two-factor authentication means you have something that you only know, and you have something else that only you have. An example might be a password and a phone that receives a text message. This allows you to confirm the identity of the person accessing the system by having two separate indicators of their identity.

The CEO believed that since users had two-factor, losing a password (or all your passwords in this case) wasn't a big deal. Even though the passwords were compromised, the hackers would have to compromise the user's cell phone as well in order to gain access.

So instead of trying to school him about two-factor authentication, I said, "Do you mind if I share my screen and we try to connect to one of these cloud infrastructure clients? It would just be like you're logging in."

Long pause, then he said, "Sure. Go ahead." I typed in the IP address. I put in the username. I put in one of the passwords that I had. And I clicked "log in."

Bam! We were in the back end of his cloud infrastructure. We could see all his servers. We could see all his backups.

Just imagine what I could have done if I were a hacker. I could have deleted the backups, then ransomed all of the data on those servers. I could have even changed *his* password. All told there were 113 client environments on his cloud. Think about what a tasty morsel that would have been for a ransomware gang? Being able to infect and ransom 113 clients all at once - well over a $10 million dollar haul.

He was so surprised. I mean, that call wrapped up very quickly, because he had to go figure out why two-factor authentication was turned off inside the cloud infrastructure. He also had to figure out how to get all these passwords changed ASAP. Why the password change? Because his team was using a pattern that contained the year and a few letters and symbols that spelled out the MSPs name.

You're probably thinking, why does this happen? I mean, why would somebody turn off two-factor authentication? Was the tech who turned it off trying to bypass something or get his owner in trouble or open a door for hackers? Was there some script he needed to run in a short amount of time, and it was taking too long to log in using 2FA, so he decided instead to just turn it off?

No. It happened for one reason. Human nature.
It's human nature to underestimate future risk.

Let me repeat that: **it's human nature to underestimate future risk.**

You might be thinking, "I don't believe you." Well, do you know anyone who understands that smoking increases the risk of cancer? Of course you do. The warning is on the package, for gosh sake. But people still smoke.

Why? Because they think it can't happen to them. It's not *this* cigarette that's going to cause cancer.

How do you fix human nature? You create policies and procedures, right? Then you punish people who break them. It's pretty simple.

Well, the MSP whose two-factor authentication was turned off had spent thousands of hours perfecting policies and procedures. *Thousands* of hours. In fact, that MSP is probably way ahead of you in that department. Not only had they invested the time to create the policies and procedures they actually paid a third party to audit them and sign off on SOC2 compliance.

So why did it happen?

To answer that, I'll ask you another question: Do you ever speed?

I do. I'll let that secret out of the box.

Next question: Have you ever been caught speeding? Yes?

And another question: If you've been caught, do you still speed? Really?

I know I do, even after I've been caught, and even after I've gotten a ticket.

What's going on here? There is a really simple policy in place: the speed limit is sixty-five miles per hour. It's super easy to understand. It's three words long. It's not hidden anywhere. It's not like this policy is buried in a binder in someone's office in the back. No. This policy is posted in plain sight. I pass it three times daily on my way to work.

It's all over the place, yet you still violate the policy, and you're even proud of it sometimes. Back to me for a minute, even after I got that ticket, and paid the fine, I still speed. In fact, I drive a fast car. I mean, if you have to drive you might as well make it fun, right? What we have here is a cultural problem. This is why policies and procedures don't change behavior.

What happened at the MSP is about culture. And when you try to fix a culture problem, you can't just create rules. You've got to help your team experience moments when the danger sinks in.

You could get a penetration test. You could pay hackers to break into your network and figure out where your vulnerabilities are. Well, I'm going to save you between $32,000 and $47,000 right now, because that's how much a penetration test usually costs. Your team already knows where the holes are. They already know where they are taking unnecessary risk. Your people already know the shortcuts they took.

You could hire an MSP to be your MSSP. But who's to say that's going to keep you safe? And by the way, MSSPs are hot targets for hackers, too.

You could build a security team among your existing engineers. I've done this before. I remember when our first CISSP got his certification. I was so excited. I mean, we had a party. We paid for his training. We were paying him above market wages. And he was pretty excited too, when he left for Lear just six months later. We lost a total of four CISSPs to organizations such as Lear and GE. Why? Your MSP is just a stepping-stone to the next big gig.

You could hire a security hotshot from outside. I've done that, too. I spent the money to get the guy into our organization, but then three months after he comes onto our team one of his buddies contacts him from the Pentagon. Poof—he's gone, and so is my security program.

You could start a security committee. But a committee doesn't change culture. It might work for a day or two. It might get you through a quarterly or an annual goal. But in the end, committees stall out and get lost in their own upkeep. Just imagine if I approached you and said,

"Hey, I have an idea. If you want to increase your sales to grow your business, why don't you start a sales and marketing committee?" You think that would work out? Do you think you'd have double digit growth because you have a sales and marketing committee meeting on a bi-weekly basis?

You could buy more products. But why bother if your team is just going to turn them off?

You could stick your head in the sand and ignore the problem. But if you intend to do that, I want you to go through a mathematical exercise first. Let's say that you get seventy-five help tickets per day, and 1.3 percent of the time there's a defect. That's a low defect rate. That's lower than the one we had at my MSP.

But let's say that 1.3 percent of the time you have a deep defect, which means you get 0.975 defective tickets a day. And let's assume there are twenty working days in a month.

Now let's assume that 8 percent of the time, those defects create vulnerabilities. That would leave you with 1.5 new vulnerabilities in your environments per month.

75 Tickets x 1.3% = 0.975 x 20 = 19.5 Defective Tickets x 8% = 1.56 Vulnerabilities

Bottom line: *none* of these options are viable.

Worried? Here's what you can do. Start with your house. Analyze your computers. Make sure you have the right tools in place, turned on, and working. Then start focusing on your clients.

Where do you start? Take a look at the cyber hygiene of your engineers. You need to understand what your engineers are doing. Just imagine if you were still going on-site to examine every single computer you worked on and weren't washing your hands between computers. Think about all the germs you would move from computer to computer. This is the same thing. You're trying to analyze your team's hygiene.

What if you could just run a small utility on your computer and find out how your team is doing when it comes to hand washing?

I have a solution that makes understanding where you are and where you're headed simple. All your team does is run a small utility on its computers—this will take between three minutes and an hour. It doesn't slow anything down. It doesn't get in the way.

You might be thinking, "Well, I have people working from home." That's no problem. It will analyze the user's home environment and identify any network devices that are susceptible to hackers. There's no need to run it on a server or use administrative credentials, it can do the analysis as a normal user.

If you own an MSP, you need to analyze your engineers' cyber hygiene. You want to find out how your tools are working. If you would like to see exactly what an attacker would get to if one of your employees to be phished, go to **GalacticScan.com/Stack** and get an analysis of your cyber security stack.

CHAPTER 2
YOUR CYBER STACK

As a leader, you realize that no problem has
only one solution. Security problems don't, either.

When we think about security, many of us think about layering various
kinds of protections on top of one another, each designed to keep
criminals (or at least people who shouldn't be inside) out.

For example, you probably want to integrate prevention, detection,
and awareness in order to stop attacks before they start or, at the very
least, mitigate the effect of a breach or attack as it is occurring. In the
worst-case scenario, you also want a way to restore your systems in the
event an attack takes place and goes undetected.

It's probably not surprising that it's getting harder to protect your
network from hackers. The number of vulnerabilities out there is
growing, and networks are becoming increasingly complex. In addition,
we have tons of cybersecurity tools to choose from. Often we opt to
buy more of them simply because it's hard to understand where the
overlap lies. That's when unruly security stacks form.

Think about your layered security stack for a moment. What are you
protecting? Are you protecting your networking? Storage? Physical
servers? Virtualization? Change management? Applications? And what
about technology already in place in the field? Are you managing
more than one standard simply because your users or clients insist on
sticking to a different platform?

As you work with an increasingly diverse set of technology—and I don't
just mean routers and firewalls—you will incur greater complexity in an
effort to manage and protect your network(s). On the market right now
are more than 750 products from dozens of vendors, offering nearly
a billion and a half versions of tech installations. Think of the vendors
you deal with. Each has its own set of rules, policies, and procedures.
Each probably has its own list of best practices, too. As you're following
protocols for implementing, maintaining, and monitoring each system,
it gets easier to miss steps with each addition to your stack. Think of

how much the oversight of even small issues can add to your risks as an IT team. And how many missed steps have led to flagrant security risks on your network?

Beyond setup and implementation—which often get rushed or overlooked—what about all the information your security produces? How are you wading through and making sure that information is alerting you in real time to real issues? Speed is key to minimizing the impact of breaches and attacks. If your detection and response times were twice as fast, how much less damage would you incur?

Now think about your information spread across a variety of platforms. Do you have a way to easily aggregate everything and see that it's all working the way you expect it to? Can you gather, consolidate, evaluate, and act upon that information? Your IT team—or security team—must find a way to essentially manufacture your necessary and actionable data from bits and bytes floating around your network. And you must do all this quickly. I'm not sure that's an easy task!

Now add in the maintenance of systems—including patches—and your job becomes even more difficult. Your laundry list of security precautions will undoubtedly create a whole host of distractions— pushing you off course from your initial goal of protecting your network. As you go down rabbit hole after rabbit hole and keep track of one complex system after the next, you might fail to monitor the security of your data and consequently the true threats to it.

Maybe you're thinking, "But I've bundled my security. My security is handled by one company that I trust."

Cybersecurity professionals typically use the analogy of an onion when they describe the way a technology stack protects your business. Most of the companies selling bundled security use this analogy at least half a dozen times on their websites. They're very convincing, and at first glance the onion analogy seems to make sense. Many layers are better than one.

But an onion is composed of homogenous layers. As you accumulate a bundled technology stack, you're building layer upon layer of mainly the same stuff. You're trusting your security to a company that follows mainly one set of guidelines with one set of priorities and one mission. Essentially, you're entrusting it with the keys to your entire network.

That's what I perceive as the onion model of security. If I had the right tool—if I were able to figure out what made that cybersecurity company tick—I could cut right through all six or seven layers you're paying for.

The takeaway?
Onion security doesn't work as well as we'd like to believe.

I'm sure you're well aware of the complex tech stack you're juggling. And I'm sure you're at least starting to become aware of the three-ring-circus model that most security programs employ —several circles of activity that deliver a single outcome.

I'm not suggesting that you divest yourself of your current security practices or even your current technology. What I want you to think about is how to *evaluate* your security stack and make sure it's meeting your end goal of data security. This circus act needs a new approach in order to deliver what you're expecting.

It needs an approach that makes it easy to prioritize vulnerabilities on your network and one that lets you understand the urgency behind an issue and the risk associated with ignoring it. It needs an approach that allows you to focus on the end goal rather than the stack itself.

As you're working through the pieces of your cybersecurity platform or program, consider this final question: Do you have a way to quantify your security? If not, you might want to take some time to track what you're paying for.

Your Layers of Security

Below is a diagram of your layers of security. Basically, they form concentric rings around the center circle—your assets.

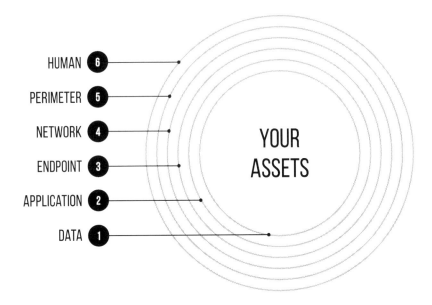

Let's start with the outer ring—the human layer. This layer is all about rules, training, and tools. Maintaining this layer requires a team of people who are equipped to keep your environments safe.

The human layer is followed by the perimeter—the layer many of us think of when we think of cybersecurity. The perimeter is where you will find firewalls, proxies, and other tools that protect the outside of your environment.

The next layer is the network layer. What are the network-layer items? Think switches, VLANs, and segmentation.

Then there's the endpoint layer. What are some examples of endpoint layer protections? Antivirus, application whitelisting, and even some SIEM products.

Next is the application layer. These are controls, such as permissions and tools that protect memory, patches, and rules built into applications to keep them safe from hackers (and users).

This is followed by the data layer controls and tools, these include items like: encryption, data loss prevention, archiving and backups.

Finally, we have our digital assets themselves, the middle ring. These are the things we want to keep secure. Within that ring, there are both super-critical assets and there are not-so-critical assets. Critical assets might include your RMM tool or your PSA tool, your documentation, your financials, customer lists, and your password tool. Those are critical, as in you must protect those at all costs. Then there are other assets that are not quite as important, such as email, chat logs, and possibly your mp3 collection. They still are valuable, but they're not critical.

The Four Functions of a Layer

Each of the layers surrounding your assets has specific tools that serve one of four functions.

- The first function is to **prevent**—i.e. to prevent an attack or another damaging event from occurring.

- The second is to **guard**—i.e., to guard against forces that cause harm. A harmful force could be an attacker or a user who doesn't know what he's doing or maybe even a disgruntled user.

- The third is to **detect**—i.e. detect suspicious activity. The idea is to identify risky behavior and block it.

- The fourth is to **mitigate**—i.e. stop any threat dead in its tracks and provide you with the ability to recover from an event.

I've audited hundreds of MSPs, and unfortunately, I see many of them skipping at least one of these layers. In doing this, you're making it easy for attackers to get through by removing some of the hurdles they have to deal with.

How does this happen? Many MSPs over invest in one layer, putting all their effort into making it very thick with overlapping tools. And then they don't have the resources or the budget to support the rest of the layers. For example, somebody who buys several antivirus programs and invests heavily in them creates an extra-thick layer that a hacker can penetrate, if he or she really understands that layer. In such cases, the data layer suffers, which creates an even bigger issue.

Let me share with you what happened in 2018 in an over investment-under investment situation.

My team and I were called to a hospital in central Mississippi in the wake of a ransomware event. The facility was completely overwhelmed. It had more than seven hundred workstations, all of which were completely encrypted, and it had around thirty or forty servers, all of which were also completely encrypted.

I won't tell you how the ransomware got in, and I won't bother telling you how much fun it was working twenty-four hours a day for twelve days straight getting the facility back up and running. We took on shifts. We worked around the clock. You know the drill.

What I *will* tell you is how the hospital got to the point where it was vulnerable.

When hospitals need help managing their data assets—specifically, their data assets associated with patient care—they often use outsourcing. This particular hospital used a cloud-based Electronic Health Record (EHR) platform to achieve this. The hospital saves money by storing all their electronic health-care records for its patients in this system, and the system keeps them safe. I'm sure you've run into situations where clients say things like: I don't have to worry about my security because I am in the cloud. I'm sure that is what these folks were thinking.

When we looked closely, we found that there was an overinvestment in two of the hospital's layers of security. The first was the human layer. If you've ever worked with a hospitals you already know they are heavily compliance driven. They usually follow very strict guidelines when it comes to caring for patients and also protecting patient data. This means there are a lot of policies and procedures, and there's a bunch of training.

The next overinvested layer was the application layer. The hospital put a lot of effort into that aspect of security, and it was able to create a very nice container that held their data. This investment went into things like being able to review all of the patient records a particular user accessed and performing audits of this access on a weekly basis.

By contrast, the hospital was under invested in protecting the edge of the network. The firewalls were not very capable, and they were not monitored. There was also no network segmentation to speak of.

The hospital also under invested in endpoint protection. There was no function that could recognize an attacker once inside the environment. When we talk about endpoints, we talk about antivirus, right?

Antivirus software has two different ways it can work. The first is signature-based, and it works just as your body's immune system does. If it recognizes a virus, it sends in the troops, and they kill the virus. For example, if you've ever had chicken pox, your immune system recognizes it when it comes in again and protects you from future attacks.

But when you get chicken pox for the first time, your immune system doesn't know what to do with it. And that's where the heuristic method of virus protection comes in: if it walks like a duck and talks like a duck, it *is* a duck. If a program is doing things that are bad, the antivirus software recognizes this. The program must be bad. The antivirus uses and acts on this information and then shuts it down.

That's where this hospital under invested. Its system didn't have any heuristic capability. All the hackers had to do was make sure their program didn't look like a program the antivirus had seen before and they were set. So the attackers changed the way their program looked and the antivirus had no clue what was going on.

Once the attackers got in, they started a second process. They blatantly named the second process virus.exe. This was a very simple program. Virus.exe did one thing. It used up all the processor time and slowed the computer down to a crawl.

Why? What do you think the user does first? He reboots his computer.

Four minutes later, virus.exe pops back up and slows the computer down to a crawl. Then the user calls the help-desk person down the hall, who wanders down to the user's computer and logs in with her credentials, because she wants to troubleshoot something, and the user doesn't have credentials to do that. At that point, the attacker gets the admin credentials for the machine! Brilliant, right?

That's the point where things go sideways: the IT person sees virus.exe. What does the IT person do? She kills it and then celebrates because she got rid of the virus. And the computer goes back to running normally.

But the attacker is still there. He still has persistence and is still able to access that machine. He now has the IT persons' credentials for the entire network. He can log into other computers, servers, hypervisors, remote control tools and even domain controllers.

The attacker then moves on from that one workstation, logs in to the server farm, and starts logging in to the servers. He does something else as he goes from computer to computer. He abuses memory and pulls any passwords or tokens that are cached on the machine.

Think about the chances of an IT person logging in to your backups from a server.

At the hospital, the hackers got access to the backups, and because the hospital was using a backup solution that was integrated with Active Directory (which is a big no-no!), the attackers had access to all the backup data. They had the domain admin account. And they had access to every computer on the network.

It was game over for the assets on that network. Ransomware won that round precisely because of these very simple missing controls.

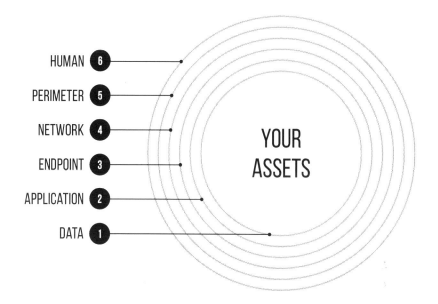

HUMAN **6**
PERIMETER **5**
NETWORK **4**
ENDPOINT **3**
APPLICATION **2**
DATA **1**

YOUR
ASSETS

What can you do to prevent this type of thing from happening on your watch? You can read on, as we go over the steps you can take to protect yourself, or many MSPs have taken me up on my offer to analyze how their stack stands up by signing up for a free consultation at **GalacticScan.com/Stack**.

For those of you who want to review your stack yourself, I highly recommend grabbing the cyber stack evaluation worksheet at **GalacticScan.com/Worksheet**.

CHAPTER 3
JUST-IN-TIME DOCUMENTATION

The first step on your journey to a more secure managed service provider is getting your people going the same way.

How do you do this? One of the most important parts is documentation. When I was the owner and CEO of a managed services provider my team was struggling to create and use documentation effectively.

How the heck do you fix that? Well we started out with a committee. We had a committee of people who met monthly to devise new articles and review articles that had problems. Our plan was to have people bring documentation that wasn't working or a list of needed documentation to our committee once a month. At certain times, when a lot of documentation was needed, the committee would schedule ad-hoc meetings to slog through the backlog of broken and needed information. Over time, this committee became a nightmare to run. We were all frustrated, and documentation was not getting into the hands of the people who needed it. Not to mention it was SLOW to get any documentation created.

The problem with this top-down, engineered documentation system? You are the constraint.

If you own the documentation process, you will inevitably create a bottleneck. It doesn't matter how many team members you have, whether you have a team of two or a team of a hundred: if you completely own the system for documenting procedures and processes—how to fix issues, what to do in specific instances—everyone will be waiting for you to fix documentation that doesn't work. You will be the one who will need to devise a way to perform undocumented tasks. The whole thing will be completely dependent on you.

It all boils down to time. If you own documentation, you could eventually have to devote countless hours to improving and documenting new items as they pop up. Let's say you delegate that ownership. Now you are paying techs and experienced engineers to create documentation rather than helping client and improving their systems.

As requests for documentation started to build up—especially as I grew my team from its original six people to the fifty-two we had when I sold the company—I realized that I needed to change the way documentation was being handled. What I needed was a way to continually create and revise our content as well as a way to quickly convey it to my team. We needed answers to pressing questions that people on the team—including some very green techs—could follow and learn from.

Some of you may be saying, "I already pay for a documentation system—someone who does documentation 100 percent of the time." That might work for you—and if it does, I wouldn't change what you're doing there.

But in my experience, if someone outside your team is providing you with documentation—especially concerning something like cybersecurity—you might struggle to integrate that person's methods with your processes, team, client base, and, most importantly, culture.

Over years of struggling to find a way to document things so my team could understand them *and* be able to turn around and improve them and validate them for our processes and clients, we needed something that everyone owned.

That's where just-in-time (JIT) documentation came in.

JIT documentation not only saved our sanity but also helped us devise new programs— including a well-oiled cybersecurity machine—with complete documentation. This documentation helped our entire team adhere to security best practices (as found in NIST 800-171).

Since I held the most knowledge within the team, I would set up short fifteen- to twenty-minute recorded calls, working with team members and explaining what I specifically wanted them to do. I would then have them create documentation as they addressed each issue at hand. Then, when team members encountered a problem, I would direct them to the documentation and have them work their way through it. The key piece here is that they created the documentation as they did the work. This allows them to create step-by-step documents with screenshots.

If there were stumbling blocks at any point, a second person (the validator) would modify the document and provide feedback to the person who originally created it. This process would continue with each person who needed that documentation or needed to solve the same problem. As the documentation was used more often, it was reviewed more often. Thus, it became better and more workable for the entire team.

For ten years I have been using this very strategy when it comes to cybersecurity documentation. JIT works because the cybersecurity field is so dynamic that relying on or creating knowledge bases from your or your guru's head simply isn't good enough.

You might be thinking, "What if the documentation isn't up to date?" Good question. When a team member finds documentation that's out-of-date, he or she invests a couple of minutes to update it and make a note to everyone that the documentation has been changed.

Finding documentation can be painful. I worried about how difficult it might be to peruse a knowledge base. Here's what I found: most of my team members did not browse; rather, they searched for the specific information they needed. This made JIT documentation work well for everyone. If the information wasn't there, they created it —and they owned it!

Getting Documentation Done Right

Let me ask you a question: Is there anyone on your team who everybody turns to when it comes to getting something fixed?

You know what I'm talking about.

I mean the wizard who knows everything when it comes to tech or maybe when it comes to your organization as a whole. You're dependent on that person. If that person isn't there, or if he's not doing what he's supposed to be doing, or if he's out sick, everything slows down.

When my MSP was earning around $1 million in revenue, we hit a spot where we couldn't grow any further. We encountered an operational logjam, and I was the bottleneck.

You see, anytime something would come to me, it would get stuck on my desk. Maybe this would be a price quote, or some sort of server that went offline, or an issue with DNS. (It's always an issue with DNS. Trust me.) So here we are, trying to figure out how to get our revenue over $1 million, and everything's getting stuck on my desk. I felt like a hamster on a wheel, working hard but getting nowhere.

Then I realized that as people were fixing issues, they were fixing them incorrectly, and that was creating security vulnerabilities. I knew the solution. The solution was to document the correct way to fix things, but who had the time?

Well, I'm going to tell you how to avoid being in that situation. I'm going to show you how you can use documentation to avoid being the bottleneck for every problem. I'm going to free you to do what's crucial to the success of your organization. Plus, I'm going to teach you how to find extra time while you're getting this documentation completed.

Think about how your documentation works today.

Maybe you spend a little time thinking about a problem that somebody's going to have. You begin to work on it, and then you realize when you're all done that you really should have documented it for the next guy.

So you stop what you're doing and go back and start again. You try to document all the steps that you might have missed along the way. This is called just-in-case documentation, or engineered documentation. Basically, you guess what people will need to solve a particular problem, and then you create the documentation for it.

The problem with just-in-case documentation? It's out of date by the time you need to use it. For example, when you're onboarding a new client and you create the new user procedure, by the time you're ready to add a new user you've changed everything in the client's environment, so that procedure doesn't work anymore.

Just-in-case documentation is cumbersome, and it's hard to complete. In addition, when you're finally done, you have to spend extra time having someone review it to make sure it's perfect. Does this sound familiar?

Now, don't get me wrong: there are instances in which just-in-case documentation is useful—for example, when it comes to policies and procedures. If you have regulatory pressure, or if you're worried about fulfilling your service-level agreements or even complying with obligations related to liability insurance, you probably want to have crystal-clear documentation of what you expect from your team (see Chapter 6).

What about the rest? I want you and your team to document ongoing solutions rather than inventing or engineering them ahead of time.

The new way, the better way, is just-in-time documentation. It has its roots in the Agile software development movement, and it means creating your documentation *while you're doing your work*. Let's be clear here: the documentation is created while you're doing the work. It's not created after you're done working. It's created *while* you're working.

Here's a quick example. Let's say that there are two characters in our story. I'll call the first one the Ticket Hero. The Ticket Hero is the person who's going to solve the problem. He's the person who actually gets the inbound issue. Maybe he's the help-desk engineer or maybe it's his project. You probably know somebody (or somebodies) like this. He's the person doing the work.

He's probably going to talk to another person in your organization for help. Let's call her the Knowledge Guru. This person is the brains behind the operation. This might be you or this might be the owner of your company or it might be somebody you always turn to for help.

Here's how just-in-time documentation works. Someone submits a helpdesk ticket. Maybe one of your clients submits a ticket for a slow printer. The Ticket Hero grabs the ticket and starts working on it, and then when he runs into an issue that he doesn't know how to solve quickly, he spins his wheels for quite some time. I didn't say he couldn't solve it—that's important. He ran into an issue that he couldn't solve quickly because he doesn't know all the steps involved in taking care of it.

He's going to have to do some research and really dig in his heels and figure this out. Now, this is one of the things that a lot of engineers have a hard time with.

New engineers, green engineers, always feel like they can solve anything. One of the issues in IT operations is that we must get people to let go of that that mind-set and start asking for help so that we can get them used to looking at documentation. So it's important to make it easy for people on your team to ask for help if they can't solve the issue quickly. You will have to define what quickly means for your organization. I used 15 minutes, as in, if the ticket hero could not solve the issue within 15 minutes he had to get help.

So far, the Ticket Hero does the right thing by realizing that it's going to take him a long time to solve the issue. He reaches out to the Knowledge Guru for help, and the Knowledge Guru explains how to solve the problem. The Ticket Hero then documents the steps the guru gave him while resolving the ticket. He documents the steps that the Knowledge Guru gave them *right then and there*: this is critical. You can't wait until you're done: you need to document as you go. It doesn't matter what platform you use. The process is the same. (You will also want to make sure the Knowledge Guru doesn't just get annoyed and solve the issue themselves.)If you do this, documentation doesn't become a burden. It's part of the process of working on an issue.

When the Ticket Hero is finished, he sends the documentation to the Knowledge Guru. Now, this is where I bet you're thinking that you have to have the Knowledge Guru look through the documentation. Don't do that!

If you do, you're wasting time, because the Knowledge Guru already knows how everything works. Looking through that documentation won't create additional value. The Knowledge Guru gets the documentation back is to have a link to it and confirmation that it was written and to be able to send it to the next Ticket Hero if she gets asked for help.

Think about that for a second: authority over and ownership of the documentation is put squarely on the shoulders of the Ticket Hero. The Knowledge Guru has a vested interest as well, she knows that documentation will set her free from the constant flow of interruptions. Just-in-time documentation will make it easier for her to do her job and avoid becoming a bottleneck. When she gets this right the team won't need to bother her over and over throughout her day.

When the issue comes in again and the Ticket Hero doesn't remember how to solve it, the Knowledge Guru just points the Ticket Hero back to the article. And here's where just-in-time documentation gets really cool.

As the Ticket Hero works through the issue, he reviews and revises the document. By so doing, he makes it more usable for the next person. He might add more and/or better screenshots. He might change the way something is written. He might even put in a new warning. Think of this as a process of continual improvement.

The idea is not to spend a bunch of time on documentation. It's to build a library of articles with lots of screenshots and make it easy for people to get the information they need.

After the Knowledge Guru reviews the Ticket Hero's results, they've completed a full cycle of just-in-time documentation. And this cycle will repeat itself over and over and over as you build your library of documentation.

As I said, there are a couple of areas where just-in-case documentation is important, especially in policies and procedures—for example, a password policy. You want to proactively tell your team why a password might need to be a certain way.

Another example might be templates. When I was running my MSP, one of the hardest things to do was onboard a new client. I was very proud of our process because we would be able to onboard a new client within ten days, which is amazing given the fact that most of our onboardings supported companies as large as 250-users. How did we do it? Part of it comes down to a combination of just-in-case and just-in-time documentation.

Let's say you have a new client. And you're going to use your new-user template for the new client. The template, which was developed using just-in-case documentation, has everything in it that a new user might need for your organization. You might have a Microsoft 365 account. You might have an Active Directory account, or you might set up the client's account in the phone system. You may have to set the client up in an HR system or a two-factor authentication product. The template will list all the things that are possible.

When your client contacts you about adding the first user, your Ticket Hero reaches out to Knowledge Guru, and she gives him the new user template. Then he makes a specific document for that client based on the template, which provides all the pieces he needs. Now he's creating just-in-time documentation.

The new-user just-in-time documentation will include screenshots and very specific links to the client's HR system and all the details you need to create a new user in that environment. It's important that you're not creating just-in-case documentation with all that information in it. Why? If you onboard the client in ten days and create a bunch of just-in-case documentation, and on day 30 you implement a new server stack or maybe a new HR system or a new ERP system, you have to go back and update your just-in-case documentation that may have not even been used.

Just-in-time documentation allows you to avoid that kind of rework and saves you a lot of time.

There's one last thing I want to mention. How do you get people to look at your documentation? How do you get them involved? How do you get them to do this stuff?

That's the hardest challenge you'll have to face. Some people will jump right in, and get started. However, there are people in your organization you'll need to convince. Tell them my story—tell them that around ninety days after we implemented just-in-time documentation, I went from being super stressed and not having enough time to get anything done to being able to get through my day without constant interruptions.

We also learned that we had to have people measure their documentation. What metric could you use in your organization? We used the number of articles we created in our documentation system as well as the number of articles we updated in the system. I used to have our team review that number every day. I will talk more about this later, but it kept us from forgetting about documentation and falling into our old habits.

Obviously, there are ways to game the system. Somebody could simply touch a bunch of articles. Yep, that happened to us along the way. You'll quickly realize that those people don't share your core values. And you'll free them up to go somewhere else, where they can game other systems.

You, on the other hand, will slowly build a system that will take the burden off your Knowledge Gurus. The first year we implemented just-in-time documentation, we created 2,026 articles. That's a lot of documentation. But the flip side is that we updated more than four thousand documents, many of them several times. This is what I'm trying to persuade you to do inside your organization.

Now for a two-part mission. Part 1: I'd like you to create your company's document about how to document. If your organization already has one, update it. I want you to use a just-in-time process for this.

Those of you who don't have just-in-time documentation in place might as well define how and when you're going to use it. Where will your documents be stored? How much detail will you expect from your team? You're probably thinking, "Wait a second, Bruce: you didn't talk about detail at all. You just talked about the process. Why didn't you talk about how much detail I'll need?"

Well, that's part of figuring this all out. My recommendation is to put in just enough detail to get the job done.

Your goal is to communicate. Communicate with your team and your future self—the one who forgets how this works three months from now.

Here's a little more info on how much detail you will need:

- First, you are going to want to add a section for warnings. I often see warnings embedded in the middle of documentation. I'd suggest you put these at the top, where they're visible. For example, put "Make sure the server is backed up before upgrading the software" at the very top of the document in addition to putting it where it falls naturally in the document. Another example is "Do not email passwords." If I put that at the very end of a document for a new user, there's a chance that person might go through all the steps, send the email, and then read the warning.

- Provide context—i.e., why a particular step is necessary. What's the purpose of this step?

- If there's a consequence, put it in: What happens if this step doesn't get done? What is the outcome if this step is skipped?

- In addition, you should assume a basic level of knowledge of your system. For example, you don't have to tell somebody how to create a new user. You don't have to tell people to click "start," go to "administrative tools," get out the admin console, and so on. You don't have to go through all that detail because knowledge of that detail is part of the basic requirements for a technician job. You do have to tell them to get the admin console and take a screenshot of it.

Trust me, you will get better at this as you go, but this should be a good start. Remember, focus on providing the level of detail we found necessary to do the job.

The biggest key to ongoing success with documentation is measurement. I suggest that each of your engineers share the number of documents created or updated in your daily huddle. Maybe you already do this with ticket closes. But documentation is just as important as ticket closes if you want to avoid getting completely bombarded with questions and get to a point where you have everything documented.

Finally, part two of your mission: I would like you to create documentation about your just-in-time process. For example, maybe you're creating a process for a new user, or maybe you're creating a process for setting up a firewall. Whatever it is, create two documents instead of one. The first document should be about the process itself —e.g., "I'm setting up a firewall." The second one should be about the process of writing the document about setting up the firewall.

Once that's done, hand it to somebody on your team and have that person create a just-in-time document for something he or she is working on. Ask that person to also update and contribute to your existing just-in-time document about how to produce documentation.

CHAPTER 4
PASSWORDS

As I was writing this chapter, another cloud provider released a statement about bypassing two-factor authentication. I thought, "What a timely introduction to the world of passwords!"

What I concluded from that statement was that if you didn't have good credentials, cloud providers aren't exactly protecting you with their two-factor authentication.

This comes on the heels of a prominent two-factor authentication provider warning that if you use their default settings for your servers, attackers could bypass two-factor authentication if the server lost network connectivity. That means fail to open, I guess. So what does this mean? A hacker can very easily get past your two-factor authentication by disconnecting your server from the internet. A great way to do that would be to just flood your DNS or poison your DNS.

What's going on? Two-factor authentication doesn't necessarily 100 percent protect you. It's very important to have it, and I don't want you to use its vulnerability as an excuse to employ a single factor solution, but be aware that it's not ironclad.

What's more? The dark web. It has your passwords. I'm sure it has your kitty photos too. If there are still some of you who don't quite understand what the dark web is, let me explain.

There are around fifty-seven billion pages on the internet. And those pages are mostly indexed by a search engine. Those pages are represented by the little yellow circle at the top of this page. If you can get to it on Google, it will show up in that little circle. That's called the surface web. That's where you guys are all looking up solutions for your clients.

Then we have the deep web. This is stuff that's not indexed by search engines. It's usually behind some sort of firewall, paywall, or password. Examples include your Facebook account information and your bank account. That all falls under the category of the deep web.

Finally, there's the dark web. That's the anonymous underbelly of the internet. That's the area where you must use Tor or another anonymity network to access. You can't get there with Google.

The simplest search engine on the dark web right now is something called Candle.

Notice that you can't really tell where that URL is, exactly. That's part of the reason it's so difficult to find stuff on the dark web: its URLs don't have very much meaning to a human.

Why am I telling you all this? Because I want you to understand that there are a lot of passwords and data for sale on the dark web. In fact, there are 9.4 billion passwords available on the dark web right now. Just to put that in perspective, there are 330 million people in the United States. That means that there are twenty-nine passwords out there for every man, woman, and child in the United States.

Here's another way to think of it. I go to DEF CON each year. (Well except last year, thanks COVID) You can drop off three two-terabyte drives, and they'll fill them with rainbow tables and passwords for you. Think about that: six terabytes of data.

What is six terabytes of data? If 100 bytes equals one kilobyte, and one kilobyte equals two pages of typed-out text, that means that one gig would be the equivalent of around ten yards of books on a shelf and one terabyte would be the equivalent of around ten thousand yards of books on a shelf.

Six terabytes would be sixty thousand yards of books on a shelf, which means that if you bound all the pages together from those three two-terabyte drives and made a book out of them, it would be 34 miles thick from cover to cover.

Imagine how many passwords that is.

That number's growing fast. So I'm here to tell you:
your passwords are probably already on the dark web.

Many of you use tools to see if your passwords are out there and for sale. I've got some bad news for you: those tools are not 100 percent reliable. These services only uncover a small percentage of the passwords that are available on the dark web. That's a challenge we're all dealing with. And why is all of this happening?

How did this huge, huge list of passwords get out there? Well, there are a couple of ways. The first is very simple: phishing. This is a great way to trick somebody into giving you a password. It's also a great way to get throwaway passwords—you know, like the one you use at Walgreens. You all have them—passwords that you use over and over and over. You might change a couple of letters and use them on a few other accounts.

Let me tell you about one of my favorite phishing expeditions. The first thing the hacker does is send a little email that says, "Hey, you won a 50-dollar Walgreens gift card." Or "Your prescription is ready to pick up at Walgreens." The victim thinks to themselves, do I have anything at Walgreens? Then they click on the link, and it asks for their password. Then it tells them they got the password wrong.

Then they automatically—enter another throwaway password, and so this little phish harvests between one and five passwords from the user before saying, "Oh, you're not able to get in with your Walgreens account. Verify with your Facebook account," and it prompts the user for his Facebook password.

Isn't this a great phish?

Ultimately, it just pushes users over to the Walgreens technical support page, which is super busy, because obviously the company is dealing with all these people getting phished. I used Walgreens here, but we see this same phish working with Amazon, Walmart, CVS, and even Home Depot.

The other way to get passwords is to use a keylogger. This picks up everything you type on the keyboard. If you get malware on your computer, it probably includes a keylogger, and this is how an attacker grabs your credentials and everything you type.

Another way hackers get passwords is through your browser cache. Users often don't hit that "don't save my password" button. And before you know it, you've got eighty or a hundred passwords stuck in your browser cache. These cached passwords are easy to crack because the encryption used on browsers is really quite poor.

Finally, do you remember the Equifax breach? If you dig into that event, you'll find out that Equifax's server admin password was "admin." You'll also find out that it wasn't just credit cards and addresses and other types of personally identifiable information that was lost during this event. It was millions and millions of passwords as well.

You're probably wondering, "Why is Bruce going through all these basic things?" I'm going through them because as an engineer, as a technician, as somebody who helps people on your team, you must understand, keep track of, and protect your own personal data. If you protect your personal data carefully, you'll end up doing a much better job for your clients.

So what can you do?

- The first thing to do is to keep track of your passwords in a password manager.

- Don't just reuse the same password over and over.

- No patterns: don't use a password that's only a few letters different for each of your sites.

- Never share a password.

- Change your passwords often. Some sites might not require you to change them except maybe once a year or when they have a breach event. On other sites, you should change them once a month, or once every few months.

- Finally, use complex passwords. I suggest at least 18 characters with upper, lower, a number and some type of punctuation.

Just keep in mind that 2FA is not your savior. If you aren't practicing good password hygiene, you're only left with one factor! That means only one factor standing between you and a hacker. That second factor may only be a text sent to your cell phone. And believe me, hackers can do all sorts of things to get your texts.

Getting back to Equifax: the company spent $1.4 billion on cleanup costs when all was said and done. That's $1.4 billion, with a capital *B*. These are very expensive events. People often think it's cheaper to pay the fine than fix the stuff in the first place, but that's not true when it comes to a breach. So we need to make sure we're not complacent. We don't want more organizations having to bail themselves out on this scale.

Think of your password as a series of characters that creates a key to access your accounts. You wouldn't want a password that looked like the key below because this key is very simple. It'd be very easy to reproduce or guess.

You might want something that looks more like the keys below, which are the kind the TSA recommends for the luggage you check on an airplane. These would be much better, right?

Well, here's the problem. Even if you have complicated keys like these, if the sites where those keys live aren't secure, and if hackers can see what they fit into—which would be the hashes in this case—they can remake the keys.

Are you guys familiar with 3-D printing? When a photograph of the above TSA keys was published in the *Washington Post*, in 2014, someone figured out from that picture how to create a template for making them on a 3-D printer. This was a situation in which there were good keys but bad security. Now you might want to consider changing the key on your luggage.

The bottom line is that if a site is hacked, even if the hackers can't get to the actual passwords, if they get to the hashes they can figure out how to generate a key that can fit.

What can you do?

- **First, use sophisticated passwords.** Never use defaults. Never use anything like "admin."

- **Don't use a single password across the board**. Never use one single password or any of its derivatives for any of your personal accounts. If you look at our checklist of the most egregious errors MSPs are committing when it comes to security, you'll see that some MSPs are actually using domain admin credentials, for things like wireless passwords, for their clients. There's a lot of opportunity for password reuse inside your organization and inside your clients' organizations. Don't do it.

- Next, **never recycle passwords**. What I mean by that is: you have password A and password B, and you just swap them. You use password A one day and password B the next. That's recycling passwords, and you want to avoid that.

- The last thing you can do is super easy. A lot of your personal information is available on the internet and on social media. **Stop using real data when you put it into these forms**. You can store the fake data right in your password management system. Just create fictional responses for questions such as "Where did you meet your spouse?" and "Where were you born?" Put fake info in that spot and take note of your answers in your password manager. This will make a hacker's life much harder.

I recently received a password for an account at one of our partners' networks, and I was surprised at the password I got back because it was so simple. I decided to ask a couple of other partners about the passwords they use when they create new users.

What I'm finding is that you guys have very, very simple new user passwords. Unfortunately, you don't create random passwords for new users. You might do something like this: "!Welcome1." Or "Welcome1!." We're finding this across the board within MSPs.

Another thing I noticed is that when a new user account is created or a user password reset, you're emailing the password to the new user.

When I talk about email, I always ask people to think of it as a postcard. You know what I mean? You write the "from" address and the "to" address, then you write your message and drop it in the mailbox. Anybody who's between the mailbox and the recipient can read it.

If Bob the postman is a little bored on his break, he can look at the postcard and read it and nobody would know. The sender and recipient would be none the wiser. Sending a password or any personally identifiable information—such as Social Security numbers, credit card numbers, anything like that—over email is super dangerous and a big no-no, so don't do it.

The other thing we see is that people aren't necessarily validating users when they call in for password resets. Think about it: How do you identify users when they call in to change sensitive information? Maybe they want new passwords, or maybe they want to access certain files, or maybe they want to update their phone numbers. How do you confirm that the users are who they say they are?

Do you check caller ID? Because caller ID can be faked easily.

Do you ask them for their birthdays? I could find those in less than five minutes by searching the internet or looking at their social media.

Anybody in any organization can find a colleague's birthday because it's probably in something like the company newsletter.

So **how do you identify a user?**
That's the first question I want you to think about.

The next question is: **What constitutes a good password in your organization**? Do you have complexity enforced inside your AD—procedures ensuring that your people can't reuse passwords and policies that require passwords of a certain length?

What about your Microsoft 365?
Do you do the same thing for cloud hosted accounts like this?

Why is all this important?

If the first password a user gets from your organization—the organization that's supporting his company, that's securing his network—is something like "!Welcome1," you're sending a strong message about how you feel about security. Share this with your entire team, because it's very important: if you don't take security seriously, neither will your clients.

Here's a simple mission I'd like you to do. Find your just-in-case document about creating new users, or find the one about resetting passwords. If you don't have them, it's time to create them.

In either case, add the following information:

- What constitutes a good password?

- How will you verify the identity of the person calling your office to ask you to do something?

- How will you generate a new password?

- How will you provide that information to the user?

CHAPTER 5
CYBER LIABILITY INSURANCE

In this chapter, I want to talk about the risk
that remains after you've set everything up properly.

Let's say you've invested in a layered approach to security. You've
put in all the defenses we talked about. You subscribe to the my
theory of making sure that every layer is different and that each
layer is supplied by a different vendor (see page 26).

And then something happens.

A hacker comes along, and this hacker is really interested in
getting into either your environment or your client's environment.
We'll call it a directed attack.

Working alerts are functioning in your environment. Everything
is locked down. You have a smart firewall. You have endpoint
protection. You've got advanced threat detection. You've
implemented a whitelisting solution.

But this attacker has done his research. He's found all the cues and
clues, and he solves all the riddles you've embedded in your layers of
defense. He addresses each challenge and overcomes it. At every turn,
he makes it through undetected.

What do you think? Could this happen to you and your company?

Of course! Even though you've invested in all the right tools, it could
still happen. Even though you've taken all the right steps, and even
though you've set out to remove risk from your environment, it could
still happen. Because no matter how good a job you do, you just can't
eliminate risk. The best you can do is reduce it.

How? Well, this is where insurance comes in.

What is insurance? Basically, insurance doesn't eliminate risk.
It transfers it—for a price—to another entity or group of entities.

You package up your risk and pay somebody to hold on to it for you. That entity will cover you if risk ever becomes reality.

A great example of this is car insurance. I've used the same car insurance company for over ten years. In my book this is a set it and forget it type service.

I would start by saying that I am a great driver. In fact, I am probably the best driver in the world. (Aren't we all?) Even though I am the best driver in the world, I still have car insurance. Why is that?

In the spring of 2020, I was traveling, and my car was at the airport when Nashville was hit by a tornado. The tornado blew the hangar away, picked it up and tossed it around 150 yards through a brick wall.

Even though I'm the best driver in the world, weird stuff still happens. This is why we have to have insurance—and we haven't even begun to talk about the risk posed by other drivers. I transferred the risk of something crazy happening to my car to the insurance company. Then, when something did happen, the company paid me the value of the car.

Now, I still had to replace the stuff that was damaged inside the car. By the way, just so you know, if your car is destroyed and it has things of value inside it, your homeowner's insurance covers that. But I had to get the damaged stuff replaced, which took time. Filing claims and replacing the lost property was a lot of work.

Do you think they were super quick about replacing my car? Nope. There were lots of questions: why was it in a hangar? Do you have hangar insurance? What about airplane insurance? Will they cover it? You see, the insurance company was interested in transferring that risk to someone else as well...

By the same token, cyber liability insurance basically transfers the risk of a cyber event to an insurance company. And this is the fastest-growing, highest-demand insurance category in the world right now. But there are some problems with cyber insurance. **There's a catch**.

The traditional insurance industry relies on historical data—models and trends—to figure out which incidents are likely to happen and how much they'll cost to cover. In the field of health insurance, for example, or natural disaster insurance, there are decades and decades of data points that help the companies figure out the risk of an event and the cost of recovering from it. But those data points don't exist when it comes to cyberattacks.

Cyber attacks tend to be discrete events and studying past attacks doesn't help you figure out when the next event will hit. And the way these attacks disrupt business is different from business to business. The impact is hard to measure. There are specific evaluation points that companies can look for in terms of risks and costs for a car crash, but they can't do that for a cyberattack. Past attacks don't provide any indication of where and when future attacks will hit, and they don't give any clues about what the cost of recovery will be.

Plus, all insurance policies and providers are not created equal. I mean, if you talk to your agents about this, I have a feeling they're going to say, "Yeah, we cover that," then get really quiet as they try to figure out how the heck to sell you a policy. The biggest issue is that they don't understand this stuff, either.

It's all new to them. It's kind of like magic. It's as though it is 1950. Imagine you asked for insurance to protect something you can't touch from someone you can't see, your insurance agents would think you're trying to pull a fast one on them, right? Then you explain that this someone you can't see could be anywhere. They could even be in a different country. No one would believe you.

Why does this matter?

First of all, if you're working with a client, I want you to be able to help that client buy the right cyber liability coverage. Insurance agents don't know everything about this. You have to ask the questions, because the agents don't know what questions to ask.

In addition, somebody on your team or one of your clients might say, "Hey, I've got business insurance in place. Why do I need cyber liability coverage?" Or another client might say, "If I have cyber liability insurance, why do I need you?"

How would you respond in those cases?

What I've learned is that the analogy of health insurance works very well. Let's say you have great medical coverage. Would you take risks that would make you more susceptible to heart disease or cancer? Or would you still worry about heart disease and cancer?

I bet you would you do everything you could to stay healthy and avoid suffering from these two afflictions. Because you know they would affect your quality of life in a unfathomable way.

The same goes for a breach or ransomware attack. The insurance company might pay the ransom, or it might pay to clean up the breach, but it will still take your company at least three weeks to recover. Not to mention all the goodwill you're losing with your clients. So even if you have cyber insurance, you still must get this cyber stuff right.

Evaluating Cyber Liability Policies

When you're evaluating cyber insurance policies, there are two considerations you need to focus on. The first is coverage requirements.

Usually when you sign up for insurance, you have to fill out a self-assessment questionnaire. This questionnaire asks things like, "Do you have antivirus software installed on every computer?" "Do you have a documented and enforced patching policy?" "Do you have active, up-to-date firewall technology, such as a UTM?"

Your client has to answer these questions—or, with any luck, you will be brought in as part of that response process. And as you begin this process, you're going to realize that each of your clients has different requirements when it comes to security. Some of them may be subject to regulatory pressure, such as the kind that comes from PCI and HIPAA.

Some of them, by contrast, might not really care. These might be businesses that don't keep credit card data, or they do everything in cash, such as the local dry cleaner. Basically, one organization's requirements are much higher than another's. That creates a difficult, complex environment to manage.

To reduce that complexity, you should have one level of security that you support across the board. That level should meet the requirements of your highest regulated client—the one you use for the client whose requirements are the strictest and/or the one who is subject to the most regulatory pressure.

For example, when I ran my MSP, we always made sure that all of our processes and procedures met the requirements of HIPAA. The clients who stored healthcare data had the highest-level requirements, and if we managed all of our clients to that requirement, then we didn't have complex, tricky rules in place to differentiate one client from another. Standardization reduces the complexity of managing a diverse stable of clients.

The next consideration you have to focus on is limitation of liability. It has to be clear where your liability starts and where it ends. For example, have you ever had a client whose Microsoft 365 got hacked? Then you come to find out that the user was using a weak password and refused to implement 2FA when you asked him to or told him to. Or, even worse, you discovered that all the users were using the exact same password.

To protect yourself in these situations and others, you have to make sure that you're not liable for your clients' actions.

Exclusions

Every insurance policy will have exclusions, because insurance companies are trying to limit their liability, just as you are.
They're trying to come up with reasons not to have to pay for an event.

Some policies, for example, will exclude an attack if it's classified as an act of war. Can you imagine—a large environment is destroyed, and the insurance doesn't cover it?

In 2017, Merck's thirty thousand computers and 750 servers were infected, and all the data was destroyed. The attack was carried out by a nation-state. And the damages amounted to $1.3 billion. When its insurers refused to pay, Merck took them to court. The case is still working its way through the system.

But if you think this is happening only to big companies, you're wrong. It's happening to all sorts of organizations that are being hit by viruses developed by nation-states. The bottom line is that you don't want an act of war excluded from your policy.

Another exclusion that might show up is something called cyberterrorism. So you need to work with your agent. You might even use the term "claw back exclusion," which is the fancy legal way of talking about it. Bottom line, be careful and work with your agent to get these exclusions removed.

If you bring up the issue in the middle of your insurance cycle, you might not be in a strong negotiating position. But at the end of your cycle, when you're getting ready to sign up for next year's coverage, you might be able to negotiate these claw backs.

Service Agreements

Why does your service agreement come up when we're talking about cyber liability insurance?

Because your agreement is the foundation of your relationship with your client. If there is a question about a claim, or if there's an event, or if there's any reason for your client to get upset with you, it all comes back to this agreement. Your service agreement can either protect you or destroy you.

Have you ever gone on a sales call and met with a potential client and felt afterward like everything was good to go? And the potential client tells you yes, she'll get your service agreement approved? Then the CEO looks at your agreement and your contact comes back and says, "Well, I must have my attorney look at this," and the brakes go on.

If your agreement is written in a simple way, your client can read through it herself, approve it, and move on. So that's one important thing to keep in mind.

Below are some other common mistakes I've seen in service agreements. These are mistakes that MSPs are making across the board, whether in Texas or New Jersey or another state. Every jurisdiction is different, but these basic considerations can affect not only IT companies but other types of businesses as well.

When you say to your clients that you're a full-service IT company, that you can protect them from viruses and cybercriminals, your clients will expect you to do those things. Be careful here. We all know that it's impossible to protect ourselves from all viruses, and it's impossible to protect our clients from all cybercrime. That's why you've got to define for your clients very specifically what it is you will do. There will be limitations, and you should identify those limitations.

Don't just say to your clients, "We are a full-service IT company; we protect you from all viruses; we protect you from this, that, and the other" instead define *how* you will protect them. Because your clients will come back to you after an attack and say, "You said you would protect us from all these things."

On the flipside, if you tell a client to look at paragraph 14, subsection B, of your service agreement, where it says, "We can't protect you from all viruses"—that's how you lose that client's business. Instead, draw your client's attention to that clause and say, "Yes, I'm going to do these things, but understand that it won't always be perfect. I can't make your environment 100% secure, but what I will do for you is apply patches within twenty-four hours" or whatever else you can promise to do.

Keep in mind that some clients won't read every paragraph of your service agreement, just as you don't read every paragraph of the agreement you're presented with when a contractor comes in to repair your air conditioner or install a new one. You sign it because you need your air conditioner repaired, and the technician won't do it unless you sign. Then, if something goes wrong, some enterprising attorney will come through and say, "Oh, well, you were bamboozled." And if you appear before a judge or a jury who's ever been flummoxed by computer systems and thought, "I expected my IT guy to take care of me in situations like this," you will not gain any sympathy.

In my opinion, it's best to be up front with people. Tell them the truth. They understand; they will get it. If you tell them, "I can't protect you from everything, but I'll do my best, and here's how I plan to do it," you'll win more clients that way.

It seems simple, right? Be careful not to overpromise. Be clear as to what you will be working on and what you plan to achieve. If the client gets upset, you can say, "Here's what was supposed to happen: step 1, step 2, step 3, step 4, and I did all four of those things." You must protect yourself from being on the hook for someone else's actions. Why? Your insurance company might not cover you, even if you have an errors and omissions policy in place. Trust me, you want an errors and omissions as well as s specific cyber liability policy.

The clause below was almost included in one of the service agreements I saw. It specifies that the client will inform the provider—that's you—of any modification, installation, or service performed on the network. You might think, "That's great. That's what I want my clients to do."

"CLIENT agrees that it will inform PROVIDER of any modification, installation, or service performed on the Network by individuals not employed by PROVIDER in order to assist PROVIDER in providing an efficient and effective Network support response."

But do I want my clients to make changes to the network at all?

For me, this is a huge red flag. I don't want any clients or third parties touching the network unless I authorize them to do so. I don't know what they're doing or what they've done, what door they've left open, what password they forgot to change. So I would recommend inserting a provision in the agreement saying that your client will not touch anything in the network without you signing off on it.

And if your client does make changes, and if you do find out about it, your warranty under the agreement ends.

After that, if the client wants you to come back in, you will need to reevaluate the entire system to find out whether it's clean. Because that's your job—to make sure the network is safe—and if you can't vouch for what another person's done, then you're playing with fire.

You might end up in a situation where you'll have to say, "No one on my team made this change," and your client's going to say, "But you said that if I gave you notice, and my guy sent an email that he did this, and you didn't catch it . . ." Now you're in trouble.

Or perhaps the client needs somebody to do some heavy lifting on an ERP platform. What we used to do in this situation is very simple: if providers were accessing the network, we would let them in ourselves and monitor their activity. We'd record their session. We would make a recording of everything they did, and we'd update our change-management documentation about their activity.

You also have to tell your service team not to just let providers in and then turn their backs on them. Your people shouldn't perform other tasks, or go to lunch, while the providers are working. They have to watch. It basically comes down to not giving your providers keys to your networks.

Third-party providers should not be responsible for any device's edge —the network—without prior notice to you. And "prior notice" doesn't mean telling you after it's already happened or sending you an email at four o'clock on a Friday. However, the bigger question is, Why is the client adding anything? And why are you giving the client permission to do it? You've essentially indirectly authorized your client or some other third party (that you don't even know) to add things to the network.

Okay, now that we spent a little time talking about third parties, what do you do when the client doesn't want to do what you recommend? To protect ourselves at our MSP, we used a document called a Risk Acceptance Form. I know there are other ways to accomplish the same thing, such as decline of service—i.e., "We'll stop servicing you if you don't take this required step." Let me give you a very quick example of something a Risk Acceptance Form might say, "You accept the risk if you open your RDP ports to the outside world. This creates a high risk of being compromised, and you will pay $250 per hour for our team to address any issues related to a compromise originating from this decision"

Basically, the documents said something like, "If there's a problem, you take full responsibility for it. And then you pay me hourly to fix it." Then, if somebody happened to break into their network, you've clearly communicated the risks and consequences of their actions.

Sometimes, a conversation is good enough. Make sure to follow up with your clients to make sure they remember and it is documented. Because they'll forget. You don't want to end up in situations where you have to say, "I told you so."

Follow up with an email. Document the record. Say, "It was great talking to you today. I told you to do these five things." So when something happens, because you know something will happen—you can say, "Listen, I'm sorry it didn't work out for you. But I did warn you."

I remember one instance when we participated in a two-day installation of an upgrade for a client's ERP platform. During those two days, our engineers asked questions, watched the third party do their work, we even recorded everything, the whole nine yards. Our participation was a kind of follow-up and monitor. Well, they ended up opening up a hole in the firewall to "allow the software to register" that would have put the client at risk. Our team shut it down and stopped the project until a safe way could be identified.

Your service agreements should include provisions for this type of situation. When the printer vendor brings in a large multifunction device and installs it, for example, what is your role? Or when a medical device company installs a new X-ray machine on the network, do you require a tech to be on-site during the install to make sure the installer shadows screenshots? Or to verify that default accounts have been disabled? How do you handle those situations?

In most cases, you don't necessarily need to be on-site. A lot of devices today allow remote access. So we would say, "Okay, you're going to be adding a device to the network. We need to know its MAC address. We will issue an IP address for you. Once it's on the network, we need an administrator account so we can access and maintain it."

Okay, now that we've covered vendors, liability, and having the client accept their risk, lets dig into service level agreements. In general, you don't want to back yourself into a corner, into a place where you have no flexibility. But you want to be able to prove to your clients that you are performing. And you may even want to be able to prove to them when they're *not* performing. So you don't want to say, "We will solve all of your issues within one hour," because then you've set yourself up for failure. Instead you can talk about response time. You could say something like: "We respond to all of your phone calls within one hour."

Similarly, if you say, "I'm going to respond to this email within two hours," and it takes you two hours and fifteen minutes, the perception is that you're not on top of it. So our SLA included a twenty-four-hour email response.

How do you sell when your service agreement says you return phone calls within one hour and emails within 24 hours? You show them how your team actually responds. When I would go on sales calls, I'd call our service desk in front of the potential client. I'm sure our engineers loved this. And an engineer would pick up, I'd ask them to describe the last issue they worked on. They'd talk us through it, showing the prospect that if they called into our office they'd be able to talk to an engineer right away. WARNING: Don't do this in front of a prospect unless you've practiced it with your team.

My point is that the service-level agreement doesn't have to be the sales tool. The sales tool can be the actual experience. You show that you always respond within twenty-five minutes or even immediately. You're overdelivering and under promising!

For a quick guide to cyber liability, visit **GalacticScan.com/Liability**.

CHAPTER 6
POLICIES

As a leader, why should you care about policies in your organization? What is the purpose of having policies, and why are they important?

Having a written policy in place allows you and your team to defend your decisions. For example, a written patch policy allows you to explain why you don't apply patches as they are released as soon as they come out. If you have a policy and a procedure that details your testing protocol, you can point out that if a patch doesn't pass the test, you don't deploy it.

I'm not talking about just-in-time documentation on this one. This is not stuff that you can afford to learn as you go and document while you're doing the work. These are things that need to be in place to protect you and your organization.

You may be wondering about the difference between policies and procedures. Policies focus on the why. *Why* are you making the decisions you're making? Procedures tell people how to implement those policies. If you don't have written policies, then having procedures is meaningless. It's like putting the cart before the horse. Hospitals have a ton of policies and procedures, mainly to defend decisions they make when it comes to patient care. You want to do the same.

So how do you create your policies and procedures.

First, a quick word of caution, you might want to avoid combining policies and procedures into one document. When you combine them into a single document, with a policy at the top and a procedure at the bottom, you create a monster. Such documents are hard to maintain.

When your team is out in the field responding to an event, they need the procedure. And if they have to go digging through the policy in order to find it, it's really difficult. So I don't recommend combining policies and procedures as you're putting together your documents.

Back to policies. Think of them as the rules of the game.

When I was growing up, we often hosted Tuesday game nights. We invited the neighbors over, and somebody would be responsible for telling everybody in the room how the game works. That's a policy; it doesn't mandate a specific action or direction. It's like the rules of a board game. You're writing the rules to the board game of your office.

How do you create a policy? Do you hire an expert first?

It's always a good idea to hire somebody who knows more than you do. If you're building out a compliance program, for example, there are a ton of people with a tremendous amount of experience out there. I would never recommend against hiring a consultant.

However, I prefer to build out policies myself, and here's why.

When you make creating policy an organizational goal, you create policies that fit your company. You understand how they work, and (more importantly) you understand how to keep them updated. Your policy document becomes a living entity. It's the difference between trying on a whole bunch of jeans to find the one pair that fits and buying the ones that you know will fit.

If you do decide to hire a consultant to get started, insert yourself in the process. If your consultant goes away and writes a bunch of policy without your feedback, you might not be able to maintain his documents inside your organization.

What are you looking for in policies? You're looking for a continuously evolving document that you and your team understand and buy into. And how do you go about creating policies? Do you start by making them up? Do you just write a policy from scratch and hope it works?

The short answer is yes. Then, as time goes by and you learn, you make corrections, and the policy becomes better. Think about it this way: you're never going to get it exactly right the first thing out of the gate. You're going to use what's called a continuous improvement cycle to figure it out.

I'll give you an example. When I was running my MSP, we had a dress code. It detailed what you could and could not wear around the office. When we started, we wanted everybody to be comfortable. We thought that if you're comfortable and no one around you is uncomfortable, you meet the dress code.

Around a year later, we added a little sentence: "Please do not wear sweatpants." Then around three months later, we added "Shirts and shoes are required." Then we added "Don't wear bathing suits around the office." We dialed it in until the policy matched our expectations.

The key here is that we wrote it down, and it wasn't perfect out of the gate.

My new company is very young. Our policies are new, but we're already finding ways to improve them. No matter where your company is in its life cycle, there will always be something that needs improvement. If you just write down your policies and they sit somewhere and you never look at them again, you're doing it the wrong way.

Here's how the continuous improvement cycle works.

Have you ever heard of the traveling salesman problem? If you're not familiar with it, see the illustration below.

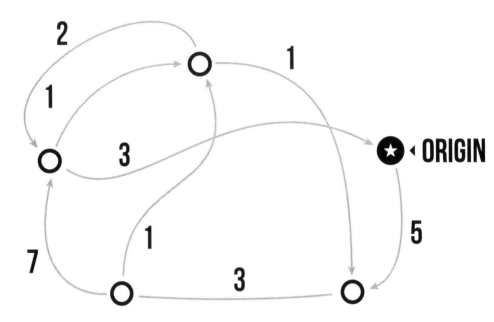

It's a classic computer engineering puzzle. You start out at the origin, and you need to stop at a number of stops along the way, and you have to make it back to the origin in as few steps as possible. Basically, you have to stop at the fewest number of points along the route.

You'll see on the illustration that there are points on each of the vectors on the path. Imagine trying to solve this puzzle without writing anything down. Just imagine that. You'd probably repeat a couple of solutions, right? You might think, "Go down the 5 to 3, then the 1 to the 7," and then you might repeat that step as you're trying it because you didn't write it down.

That's really important to remember when it comes to policies. If you start by making a map, and then test the map, and then find out what went wrong, and then improve the map, it's much easier to understand the steps you took.

The most important takeaway from this chapter is that you need to get started, write something down, and get moving. In short, when it comes to a policy:

- The first thing to do is document it.

- The next thing to do is improve it. Share it with your team. Get everybody's buy-in.

- Use the policy.

- Find issues with the policy.

- Then go back to the beginning again. Go around and around and around until you have the policy exactly the way you want it.

One way to save time and effort is to start with standards. These are created over many years, with hundreds of people contributing to them. That's years and years of continuous improvement. Standards can save you from stupid mistakes. In the case of the traveling salesman problem, you would use a standard if you consulted Google Maps to find the shortest route. It might not be the route you want, because maybe you plan on stopping for coffee along the way. But overall, it's darn close.

That's what a standard will do for you. It's much easier to start with something that's already written down and ready to go.

The standards we use include CMMC, HIPAA, and PCI. In addition, many regulatory bodies depend on NIST 800-53 and NIST 800-171. So those are the standards you can look to when you're creating your policy. But be prepared, policies are often wordy and super dry. Your eyes may not bleed by the time you are done sifting through them, but your head will certainly hurt.

I also recommend starting with a template. There are a couple of really easy templates available from the SANS Institute. They've already linked them back to an NIST standard, so that provides an easy way to get things going. The templates might not fit your needs exactly. Some of them specify Cisco routers, for example, and you might not use Cisco routers, and some of them use some very protracted language that your team might not understand. So you might be making some changes and rewriting them.

You will probably want to invest in some type of policy and procedure or document management portal. Why? First, document control, is really important. When you're building your policies, you need to be able to show exactly what your policy looks like on a given date. Let's say you write a policy, and you start using it, and then you make a change to it in January of the following year. A solution like this will allow you to preserve both the old and new versions. Essentially, it creates a map of how decisions were made.

Another benefit is that you don't need to use Word and your file system to manage these documents. You can certainly do that, but these programs are not ideal when it comes to formatting and maintaining the policy. If you're not careful, and if you're not using a tool like this, you end up having to have a policy about formatting and maintaining your policies, which turns into a big nightmare. I suggest some sort of portal that's designed, purpose built, to track policies and procedures.

When I reviewed several errors and omissions policies and cyber security self-assessment questionnaires. I discovered you should start by establishing the following four policies:

- Acceptable use

- Password construction

- Password protection

- Clean desk

Every single self-assessment questionnaire and insurance policy I read looked for these four things. Don't get me wrong. They asked for additional items, such as patching policies, but these four were consistent across the board. You might think you could roll all these out into one policy, but if you do that, you'll have one big monster document that's a pain in the rear to keep updated. I suggest you create one policy for each of these four things.

So how do you get started?

The answer is: just do it. As author Brian Tracy says, "Eat that frog!"
Do it first thing in the morning and get it over with. If there are two
frogs, eat the bigger one first.

Here's the process I recommend:

- First, find a template that you like.

- Then make some edits to it so it fits your organization.

- Then save it as a PDF and share it with your team. Ask for feedback.

- Spend some time making edits based on your team's feedback.

- Give it back to your team and get approval.

- Finally, share the finished product.

I know you might be able to sit down for a day and get it done yourself,
but if your team is part of the discussion when you're building the
first iteration—if they have a stake in helping define what they're held
accountable to—you'll have a much easier time getting everyone to
comply. The key here is to keep your team engaged AND just get it done.

One last question: Why wouldn't you delegate policy writing to somebody else? Why can't you hand it off and not worry about it? Why not make it someone else's problem? Why does the leadership of your organization have to be part of this conversation?

Remember my example of the speed limit (page 22)? People who break the speed limit do so because they haven't (yet) been the victim of an accident caused by speeding. They don't understand the danger. It's not a training problem. It's not that there are no consequences, either, because if you violate the policy, you get a speeding ticket. Yet we still speed, even after we get speeding tickets.

That's why it's so important that leadership is involved and that your policies match the culture within your organization. If they don't, there's a disconnect. You can't change behavior with a policy —even if it's simple, even if you train everybody, and even if there are consequences. It's extremely hard to use someone else's canned policies and call it a day. It takes work to make policies that fit your company and its culture. Great policies will do both.

CHAPTER 7
TABLETOP EXERCISES

In this chapter, I'm going to talk about using tabletop exercises to prepare for disaster.

But before we get too far along, remember my discussion of fire drills (page 17)? Think back, when you went through fire drills in elementary school, did they ever change the nature of the issue? No, the school's on fire, so you get the hell out of there. You get up, walk down the hall, and out the door. It's not complicated.

I want you to think of bare metal restores as being like fire drills. They're very specific: we had a major catastrophe with one of your servers, and we have to recover. That would be a bare-metal-restore situation. You might have to recover on a different cloud tenant or infrastructure, or maybe a local server blew up. But you have to recover to new, bare metal. It's like a fire drill in that it's very simple. It's very specific. It's also very technical, usually.

But a tabletop exercise is a little different. In a tabletop exercise, you're not just going through the motions. You're not just going through the technical bits. In fact, you might not even use tech at all.

Think of a tabletop exercise as goal oriented. You have a certain goal you're trying to achieve. Instead of flipping switches and pushing buttons, you sit down and discuss who's going to perform which tasks. Ultimately, the goal is: How do we make this better? How do we improve the process next time around?

A tabletop exercise is a discussion-based activity. You review your processes and find ways to improve problem areas at the end of the exercise.

Think of it this way - fire drills test your systems, such as backups. Tabletop exercises test your overall response.

So why is this important? I mean, I'm guessing no one has said to you, "Hey, you need to do a tabletop exercise." I'm bringing this up because of my experience working with health departments and hospitals in preparation for things like pandemics, hurricanes, and natural disasters. They constantly practice responding to these types of events. I'm bringing this up because this is something we should see practiced all the time in tech land, and we don't...

The tabletop practice model is what we really should be using just like these hospitals. Instead, we don't think about how people and systems need to work together in an emergency. In fact, many of the MSPs that we audited didn't even have disaster recovery plans. (Even fewer had incident response plans.)

Sure, it seems like a daunting, thankless task to sit down and create one. I've heard MSPs say things like "My team deals with disasters all the time. They'll get through it."

But here's the thing. I'm not saying you guys won't make it through a disaster if something goes sideways. I am saying that having a plan will reduce the stress on your team while they're dealing with that disaster. It will improve your results.

Maybe you'll respond faster. Maybe you'll save time avoiding a bunch of rework during the disaster itself. Maybe you'll just communicate better because your team knows who to engage. Trust me, your results will be better.

How do you do this? Well, you should have a written plan. If it's not written, you can't improve it. This goes back to that traveling salesman puzzle on page 69. If you don't have a documented plan, you won't be able to improve anything, because it's really hard to remember what your plan is ninety days or even six months later, when disaster occurs.

So how the heck do you get started?

This is the most difficult part of getting disaster-preparedness stuff together—sitting down and figuring out what should go into your plan. That can feel overwhelming.

My first suggestion is: don't assign it to a tech. I mean, most business owners say, "Oh, I'm just going to find somebody. He's going to own this, and he's going to create it."

Don't do this. Disaster planning isn't a technical problem. A technician won't be the one who fixes it. Fire drills are technical. Disasters, on the other hand, are something your whole organization will be part of.

Other business owners tell me, "I'm a one-person organization, so I don't need a disaster recovery plan. I've got everything right here"—pointing to their heads.

But whether you're a one-person organization or a forty-person company, you need to put together a plan and then go through a tabletop exercises to determine who needs to be part of your disaster and incident response. That might involve more than just the people inside your organization. You have to ask yourself, "Who do we pull into this discussion in order to make our plan successful?"

Let's talk about how to do a tabletop exercise:

- First, you start with a goal. What the heck are you trying to test?

- Then you figure out who's going to participate in the project.

- Next, you establish the rules of the game. How will it work?

- Then you go through the exercise itself.

- After that, you perform a debrief—more about that below.

- Finally, you update your documentation and training. That's why documentation is so important, because if you don't have it to begin with, you won't have anything to update.

All right, let's get started.

I suggest you keep this really simple and not super expensive. Make it something you can get done in an afternoon. Or maybe even just an hour and a half. A great time to do it is right after a two-day off-site. For example, on the second day of your team off-site, you might switch gears, drink a little coffee, and then do a tabletop exercise.

If you're one of the folks out there who is starting with, well, nothing, I've got a trick for you. Have somebody record the plan as you go. Use GoToMeeting, Teams, or whatever your favorite platform is and record it as a video call. Some platforms will actually write the transcript out for you. That's super helpful, because then you can go back, pull the transcript, and turn it into the start of your document. Or you could send the recording to somebody and have that person transcribe it for you.

To help you get started, we have a form called the annual disaster planning form.

When I do a tabletop exercise, I want to achieve three things.

First, to give people practice at critical thinking. Second, to give them experience with real-life scenarios. And third, to get them working together to follow a plan.

One final piece of advice: share the disaster scenario with your team before you get started. You might be thinking, "Well, in a fire drill, they don't reveal the day or the time beforehand. No one says, 'Hey, there's going to be a fire drill at 9:03 p.m.—be ready for it.'"

But remember that fire drills and tabletop exercises are different. Fire drills test your response to a specific component of your technology when it malfunctions. Tabletop exercises, by contrast, test your response to problems that aren't so specific. So let your people know what's coming.

Here's an example: There's a vulnerability in the RMM, and there's no patch for it yet.

What do we do? That'll get them thinking. You're trying to improve. It's not about how fast you can get something done. It is about how you get it done.

So now you've got everything ready to go, and you want to start working on the tabletop exercise. What's the first thing to do?

Set Your Goal

The first thing to do is set your goal, and that means identifying a disaster you want to prepare for. And there are a lot of disasters out there to choose from.

Some of them might have even happened in your community or your region, such as hurricanes, tornadoes, and snowstorms.

Pandemics—guess we've experienced one of those recently!

Maybe there's been a fire at your office, and nobody can get in for thirty days.

How about a denial-of-service attack on your phone system?

Or an Office 365 failure, but not one that you're used to —maybe one that knocks out the program for five days?

Here's an example of a goal you can use for your first tabletop exercise: test the team response to the RMM being down. That is, how will your team respond if they don't have access to your remote monitoring and management tools? What would that look like?

Let's say there's a vulnerability exploited in the RMM, and you come to find it doesn't have a patch yet.

Now what do you do?

There are a lot of questions you have to start answering, including, "Have any MSPs been attacked using this vulnerability? How many people have been hit?" "Can we use our firewall to lock everybody out?" "Can we lock our own clients out?" Those questions will come up naturally while you're talking through the event. And the answers may be things that you want to add to your plan when you are done with your exercise.

You also want to choose a disaster that you can escalate. Let's say everybody gets through the first part in ten minutes and you're thinking, "Oh, gosh, now what?" Well, escalate it; make it harder. Think about what else could happen. For example, suppose the hackers who attacked your RMM also deployed ransomware to two of your clients. Now what do you do? Maybe they deployed it to ten of your clients. What do you do then?

Choose Your Participants

After you have your goal set, the next thing you do is choose who's going to participate in the disaster response. Who will be the people involved in the tabletop exercise?

You might think, "I'll just get my technical team involved." But that's not the best way to do this. You might also think, "Maybe I'll just get my leadership team involved." Again, that's not the best way to do this.

You want a mix of people. You want a couple of tech people, maybe somebody from marketing, maybe somebody from your leadership team. You may want to include vendors, especially those you rely on from a restore standpoint.

You might also want to involve clients. Maybe you have some clients you really trust. If you're a one-person organization, you're surely going to depend on your clients and vendors to help you during a disaster. And being part of the planning will make them better at responding when there's an actual event.

Establish the Rules

The next thing to do is establish the rules of engagement.
How do you conduct your tabletop exercise? I suggest the following.

- First, **no interruptions**. I don't care if the house is on fire.
  We're not leaving. We're going through this entire session together.

- **Practice the Golden Rule**. Treat people as you want to be treated.

- This is a learning experience, so **keep it fun**.

- **Don't be an asshole**. The more seriously you take this scenario, the better the results, and if you cheat or cut corners, it won't be effective.

- Finally, **keep the exercise on schedule**.
  That's going to be important in an actual disaster scenario.

Conduct the Exercise

So you've set the goal, chosen who's going to be there, and made the ground rules. Now what?

Now you get everybody in the room or get everybody on a call or a video chat. You describe the scenario again—because you've already shared it with the participants before the meeting—and then ask everyone to describe how they would respond.

Keep track of what's going on with the scenario as you escalate, and communicate those escalations.

I also suggest a bit of role-playing. For example, if one of the steps is to call your clients and let them know that you have to turn off your remote monitoring and management tools, practice the phone call. Get some feedback on what that phone call should sound like. When you are done you will want to add this script to your plan.

If you plan to send an email communication, get the communication together and talk about what should be on it. The whole purpose is to go through all the details.

For example, if you plan to turn off all access to your remote management tools, make a list of what will be affected. How will you do that? Who will do it? How will you notify your team?

Debrief

After you go through the exercise, take a break for half an hour or so, then discuss the results. Following are some good questions to ask. They're pretty straightforward.

- First, **did you have the right people in the room?** Did you have to pull in others who should be on a disaster-response team?

- **Were the tools that you had in place adequate?** Or was there something that would have been good to have on hand?

- **What about communication?** Did you do well with internal and external calls and emails?

- **Should you have had a template to work from?** Should some procedures have been templated in case you had to issue a mass communication on the fly?

- **How did you do from a timing standpoint?** Did you complete the exercise in a reasonable amount of time? Or was it way too lengthy?

Update Your Documentation

Finally, after you've discussed the results, you should update your documentation.

I know I've said that you should practice just-in-time documentation—that you should update all your documentation as you're working. But during a tabletop exercise, there might be some things you don't know how to fix at that moment. If that's the case, just document the issue and take it to your next weekly leadership meeting.

The last thing I want to mention is your mission for this chapter. I want you to record the date on which you're going to go through your first tabletop exercise.

Remember, you should take only around an hour and a half for the actual event. Then you take a half-hour break. That break is critical. Then you spend around forty-five minutes discussing the results and updating the documentation. We're talking no more than an afternoon. If the meeting runs longer than that, it starts to lose its value.

Once you've gone through a tabletop exercise for your disaster response plan, consider doing one the next quarter for your incident response plan.

If you're interested in an example of a tabletop exercise every MSP should be conducting at least annually, visit **GalacticScan.com/Tabletop**.

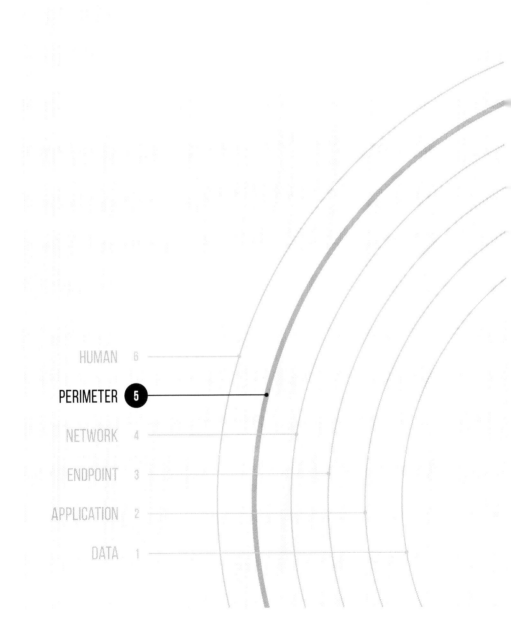

HUMAN 6

PERIMETER ⑤

NETWORK 4

ENDPOINT 3

APPLICATION 2

DATA 1

PERIMETER

The perimeter is perhaps the layer of your cyber stack that doesn't get enough attention. But if you define your perimeter correctly and fortify it with technology that works (think configuration and testing here), you will in theory have a well-protected fortress. The problem is that we rely mainly on one form of perimeter and fail to realize how that outer shell is not as hard or impermeable as we might think. We also miss all sorts of holes in our externally facing business. That's why I strongly believe that when you think about your security, you should think not only about devices and firewalls but also think of everything that is facing the outside world.

CHAPTER 8
FIREWALLS

When I discussed cybersecurity stacks in chapter 2, I talked about filtering, firewalls, DLP, IPS and IDS, antivirus software and log aggregation. Now I want to spend some time talking about best practices—the things you should put in place for firewalls and the types of clients who are willing to invest in them.

Sales

When we talk about firewalls, we need to talk about the sales side as well as the security side, because if we don't know who values this type of security investment, and we try to sell it to the wrong type of client or recommend it to the wrong type of client (in my world, selling and recommending are the same thing), we'll end up with clients who don't aren't getting the security that they need or want in place.

First, let's get to know the various types of MSP clients.
I like to classify them into three large buckets.

- **The Basic User:** The first bucket includes clients who are interested only in basic security. These are the people who want nothing more than your simplest solution. They don't want to invest in special security measures. They may not want to invest in training. They don't want to invest in policies and procedures.

  These clients aren't subject to regulatory pressure, and they're often very, very small businesses. You can educate a basic security client, but it will take a lot of time and investment, and at the end of the day, you may very well end up not making those clients any more secure than they were when they started (that is, unless you're going to cover the bill for everything while not making any of their processes more complicated from added security measures. I would recommend against this unless it makes your work easier or reduces your risk of having to spend time cleaning up an incident).

- **The Security-Conscious:** Another type of client is security-conscious. These clients understand that there are real threats out in cyberspace. They're interested in protecting themselves and are willing to invest in the effort. These organizations are worth your time; they are interested in your recommendations and want to be part of the discussion.

- **The Compliance-Driven:** Finally, there are compliance-driven clients. These clients are under pressure from regulations such as the Sarbanes-Oxley Act—usually, they're large organizations and publicly traded companies. You might also be dealing with industry-specific compliance requirements, such as those imposed by the NCUA for credit unions and the FDIC for banks. FINRA falls in the bank area as well. CMMC, maybe PCI-DSS. Or HIPAA for health-care organizations. There are all sorts of regulatory pressure on compliance-driven clients.

  Here's the good news about compliance—it generally all relates back to NIST standards, so if you understand these, you can service a wide variety of clients who have regulatory issues. This means you can sell a single compliance package to clients regardless of industry—that is, if you plan your stack and security strategy accordingly.

Now let's talk about how these three types of clients relate to your firewall.

The bottom line is firewalls need care and feeding. And if you can explain that to your clients—if you can clearly articulate the type of care and feeding required—you can help them understand why they have to invest in them. For example, you can tell your clients that if they invest in the right areas of their security stack—specifically, in the perimeter—it decreases their downtime and it saves you effort. It's a win-win for everybody involved.

When I was running an MSP, we were charging between $150 and $800 per month to manage a single firewall. It is a best-practice charge for firewall support and maintenance. I found, that in order to put the required effort and upkeep in when it comes to firewall support, maintenance, and monitoring you'll need to charge for it. Don't just pass through the license cost, because you will find that you have a lot more work on a firewall then updating the licenses.

I discovered that the best way to persuade clients to upgrade to a managed firewall is to keep the conversation simple. What I said was, "You know, this security stuff is changing all the time. Hackers keep getting better, and the way you're doing business keeps evolving. The amount of effort required is also changing, and the tools we need are increasing in cost. We have to talk about adding something called a firewall, a smart firewall, to your environment."

But I want to warn you, don't imply you're monitoring their firewall 24-7 if you're not. You'll want to make that really clear. You can say you're monitoring it. You can set up alerts that get your teams attention when something bad is happening, and you can explain how your alerting system works. This way they are not expecting you to have eyes on glass all night long.

Standardization

All that being said, probably the most important thing you must do when setting up your firewalls is standardize. What do I mean by standardization?

Providers

Well, you don't have one-size-fits-all clients, right? Even though that isn't the case you will want to keep your firewall selection simple. You will want to focus on a single firewall provider for all of your clients. You might get stuck and have to choose two providers, but never, ever, ever go over two. If you can use only one, that will make life simplest and best for your growth. I know this because at my former MSP, we had three providers for a while, and it was just too much to handle, too difficult to deal with. When you hire a new person they have to learn three different devices, they have to learn three different support paths. Worse? You have to manage three different patch cycles. Keep it simple, you will thank me later.

Hardware

The next thing you should do is standardize your hardware. Narrow it down to three or four models. You don't want to service all twelve models that a vendor has.

Why? Let's start with support. It is easier when your team knows what the hardware looks like because they see it all the time. Next, hardware breaks. These routers aren't usually something you can just go to the local store and replace. It's a good idea to store and have on hand one or two of each of those models, and you don't want to have to store twenty pieces of hardware. In fact, that can be one of your selling points to your clients: if they ever have a problem with a piece of hardware, you'll have a "hot spare" (or a "warm spare," whatever you want to call it) in your office ready to go. You can bring it out whenever lightning strikes.

Standardize your hardware to three to four models, have spares in your office, and make that part of your value proposition. It's yet another reason why your clients should move to the managed-firewall level of service and why they shouldn't just buy their own hardware.

Firmware

Okay, so you have your new router. It came from the manufacturer with a standard firmware load. Is that good enough? Nope. The first thing you are going to want to do is get it to the most up to date stable version of the router manufacturer's firmware. Most of these devices allow you to download the firmware as a binary. You will want to do this so you can come back and apply this very same version of firmware in the future. This will be your standard firmware for deployment. As in you will not just go and download the latest version of the router firmware every time you deploy. Instead you will use this one. Why? The next step is creating a standard configuration. You will want to have that configuration applied against the same firmware. Trust me.

Configurations

The next thing to do is standardize your configurations. Here's how I recommend you do it, because when I first started this posed a challenge for me.

First, if it takes you longer than an hour to set up a firewall, you're doing it wrong. You can still bill a client for $800 to $1,000 to set it up, but it shouldn't take you more than an hour—because you should have all the settings ready to go beforehand.

Here's an example: I want you to set up a failover port on each of the routers you deploy, even if the client isn't going to have failover. Set it up anyway. Set up the port monitoring to make sure it's online. Set up IPS and IDS rules. Set up rules for things like web filtering—things you see all the time in your environment.

And then stop. Stop right before you put in your clients' IP addresses and other specific information. Stop and save what you put together because that will become your standard configuration. That will become the template you use going forward for every deployment. I used to get this wrong, by spending a ton of time figuring out what should be in that template. Just create the template on your next deploy.

Notice that we did this the same way we did the just-in-time documentation. We didn't make a template today because we think we're going to sell a firewall next week. We made a template today because we're rolling a firewall out now, and we're going to create and save that template. Then, as part of the process, you load that template, then you update the client specific settings the way you need them to be.

Updating Firmware

Okay, the next step is going to be updating your firmware to the latest version. (Unless this is your first router deploy with this template, you may be a few firmware versions behind. Reminder, you don't want to apply your router configuration template to the latest firmware. You will be applying it to your standard firmware version.)

You're probably thinking, "That's an obvious one," but we're seeing a huge increase in events related to firewall firmware not being up to date. You might also be thinking, "Well, it's not a big deal, because we block access from everywhere, except one IP address in our facility."

Or you're thinking, "Patches come out all the time for computers. It's the same thing. We'll get around to it when we get around to it." But this is very different, because this affects the perimeter of the network. And when attacks affect the perimeter, they can be devastating.

Here's an example of a recent exploit. All you have to do is type in **HTTPS:// [the IP address of the firewall]. I use VPN.[your company]. com/remote/fgt_? lang = /../.**

Put this string into your web browser and hit Enter from anywhere in the world, even if your client has limited remote access. You will then be able to access a list of every user who's ever logged in to this firewall using the SSL VPN and have their passwords in the clear.

At my former MSP, we used this string when we were doing a penetration test, to get all the passwords for an organization so we could get into its VPN. And guess what? When the client had RADIUS authentication set up, which was pretty often, we were in! Not only did we get the passwords for the VPN, we got the domain passwords, too. So if you're running a version of firmware that's over six months old, it's time to update. Check with your provider for the latest patches and get them applied.

And that brings up the next point: Are you running a bunch of different versions of firmware on your devices?

I see this mistake pretty often. You might have routers in the field that are running all sorts of different versions of firmware. This creates problems when it comes to support, because buttons move, features change and even command line gets updated between versions of firmware and some firmware runs better than others.

Get all your clients on the same version of firmware. One way to go about this is to test it at your office—eat your own dog food, as they say. Test it each time a new version comes out. Drop it on the router at your facility, and you can troubleshoot it locally if there's a problem rather than having a client down while you drive out to their site and fix it.

Testing

The last element of standardization is testing. Standardize the way you test a firewall every time you roll it out. You're welcome to test using our tools. They will let you know whether antivirus and IPS / IDS are working. The key here is to inspect your work when you are done.

One more warning, always, *always*, always have a testing plan in place to test your alerting and your failover to make sure they work. Another suggestion is to test whether you can log in to the administrative console from your management network and whether you can log in from other points across the internet. Test, test, test. When we evaluate networks, we can tell which MSPs are testing, and which ones are assuming everything is working. One other word of advice here: make sure you have some type of ongoing testing. As in, whenever someone makes a change on the device, they have a plan to test it.

VPN Traffic Filtering

If a VPN user connects to the VPN, you want that user to have access to a specific resource or server stack and maybe a printer or two, but that's about it.

Do you really want the VPN user to be able to access the computers inside the network? Unless you are using them for remote control, the answer is absolutely not. And those computers—you don't really want them to be able to access the VPN computers, either. That's what filtering is all about—segmenting among the various VLANs your assets are set on, making sure that VPN access only goes to the very specific points it should go to. Making sure computers that people log into don't have full access to all of the servers in the environment.

Why is that important? Because sometimes VPN users don't have as much security in place as the assets inside your facility do.

IPS and IDS

The next thing you need to deal with is IPS and IDS.

You'll hear me standing on a soapbox about why IPS and IDS are so important. Sure, it's annoying that they are *always* changing. If you aren't paying for a subscription from one of your vendors that is updating your IPS and IDS solution at least daily, you don't have this set up right. This is because you need rules like the ones below. This is the list of rules that was released by Snort, an open-source IPS engine. Snort is free. You can download it and play with it to your heart's content, and it allows you to see whether somebody's in your network. A lot of firewalls use it as their IPS and IDS engine.

Why is that important?

In the summer of 2020, hackers realized that they could set up a server—a DNS server to be specific as a command-and-control network. They produced responses over DNS through TXT records. This was particularly mean, because most people in information technology have a hard time with DNS. This tactic also caught a number of people by surprise, the attackers were able to pull information out of your network or control devices in your network using the system everyone uses to find their way around the internet. If you're not using IPS and IDS, and one of your users gets phished, you will soon be leaking information through DNS.

By the way, all those compliance-driven clients, the ones who have to conform to HIPAA or PCI rules—they all require an IPS or IDS in place as part of that NIST rule set.

Antivirus

Yep, you can turn on antivirus at the firewall level on most of these devices.. It's kind of like having an electric fence around your property—a good way to prevent someone from coming in. If you just have an alarm inside your house that goes off when somebody cracks the door open, it doesn't prevent the intruder from coming all the way in. Yes, it detects the entry and could mitigate the response, but it doesn't prevent it from happening in the first place. That's why antivirus is a really good thing to have in the firewall. Just a little more proactive than on the endpoint.

You will also want to set up your antivirus and to get alerts sent to you. You are specifically looking for outbound traffic that contains malicious payloads. Think about it, if you block something inbound that is good. You kept someone off your turf. If you are blocking outbound traffic, you have an indicator of compromise. Someone is inside your network trying to get out. One of your devices is already compromised.

Limit Admin Access

It's also very important to limit admin access.

On one occasion, I was performing a network assessment for an MSP, and I was able to crack a whole bunch of its passwords. These happened to be passwords we cracked on one of the help-desk engineers' computers. All told, I found around twenty-five firewall passwords. I could tell that they were firewall passwords because they had the external IP address and the firewall admin information embedded in the URI.

I got the owner of the MSP on the phone and went through the results with him and pointed out this problem. He said, "Yeah. We use two-factor authentication, so it's not a big deal."

Here's the catch. Most firewalls don't have two-factor authentication available yet. With his permission, and while he was on the phone, I connected to the first three firewalls—from my computer in my home—and was able to get on his client's network. I could have opened up port 3389 to one of its RDS servers or stood up a new VPN for future access. It was wide open.

This is why you'll want to limit admin access.

I recommend that you limit admin access to only one computer in your environment—maybe a terminal server your team only uses for managing firewalls. You'll have one computer in your environment that has access to your client's administrative interface, and that's it. This allows you to avoid a situation in which somebody gets a bunch of passwords or even cracks a network remotely by just trying password after password.

Limited admin access is something you should embed into that template I was talking about above, so you don't have to remember to set it up every time.

Automated Backup

The final thing you want to implement is an automated backup system.

On a monthly basis, get a backup of all the settings on the firewall, just in case Lightning strikes or the firewall forgets what it was doing. Firewalls can be tricky beasts. They may run for months or years, you may apply firmware to them multiple times with no issue. Then one day, they just stop working, if you have a backup of the configuration, you will be able to use one of your spares and have everything up and running quickly.

If you can't do that, make it part of your quarterly business review process. Either arrange for a ticket to be automatically created for somebody to back up the firewall or create a quarterly business review check list that includes this process. Then tell your client that you've backed up the configurations for the perimeter network devices.

This might also be a good time to back up some other configurations, such as switch configurations and virtual machine configurations.

We've been working with our partners and colleagues to figure out what needs to be included in a firewall checklist to make sure our clients' alerts are working. I can't believe how many MSPs we've audited fail to get their firewalls to alarm when we simulate ransomware attacks within their environments.

If you'd like a copy of the ransomware-proof firewall checklist, visit **GalacticScan.com/Firewall-Test-Checklist**

CHAPTER 9
WEBSITE HARDENING

In this chapter, I want to talk about the things you need to consider when you're protecting your reputation.

I've already talked about the various tools you need to have in place to protect yourself from hackers. You're probably thinking, "I'm doing all the right things here Bruce, I got this." That's great. I want to discuss a different type of risk. Getting this wrong won't get you infected with ransomware. You won't suffer a public pants-down spanking in front of the rest of the community. Instead, you might be slowly losing business prospects or clients without even knowing it.

Imagine that you've been working with a potential client for months. This is a big opportunity. It's definitely going to be lucrative because they have their own IT team. You will just be providing high level support, monitoring, and security services. You won't have to do the help desk, so you can focus on the higher end items your team likes and won't require as many different types of labor. Seems like a great win.

You've done everything right. You started by performing a cybersecurity assessment. You uncovered all the issues. You showed the prospect how their current security solutions are asleep at the wheel and not picking up on advanced persistent threats inside the environment. You have the CEO on board. You talked to the IT director. She's interested, and you even got the budget approved. This deal is ready to go.

Instead of getting a signed contract in your email inbox, you get a message from the CFO. It says they won't be moving forward.

In fact, it goes on to say that the team took a look at the security of your organization. They looked at your website specifically. They noticed some things that made them nervous. They discovered that you're not doing the things you're telling them to do. They saw this one data point and decided that you're not protecting yourself. They concluded, if you are not protecting yourself, or you are overlooking issues on your end, you'd miss items on their network.

I'm sure you've heard this before: your marketing is the only thing prospects know about your service before they buy. When you're talking to prospects and you tell them that your service is good, your marketing is the only thing that proves it to them. People don't really know anything else about your business before they start doing business with you. Well, I would add one more thing to that.

It's your marketing *and* your external security posture that communicate information about your service. And it's not just prospects who look at this stuff. Current clients and vendors look at it, too. If you decide to engage a new insurance company, for example, executives there will make sure your security posture looks good. They will do this by scanning the outside of your network, your DNS and even your website. This is the fastest way for them to measure; they don't have time to inspect every one of their clients from the inside of their network.

So I'm going to take you through the seven things you should have in place in order to align your external security posture with all the hard work you're doing to improve your internal security stack and harden your security solutions.

1. Enable multi factor authentication everywhere.

2. Back up everything.

3. Evaluate your DNS.

4. Learn what to put on your website and what not to put on your website.

5. Prevent brute-force attacks.

6. Audit your certificates.

7. Polish your business facade.

Now let's get started.

Enable Multi Factor Authentication

You're probably thinking, "Bruce, I've already enabled 2FA. I've got it on my backups, my administrative accounts, and I have it in my Microsoft 365." And you're right. Those are things you have to enable 2FA on.

But is it enabled on your website? How do you keep attackers from gaining access to that? If you're using WordPress as many of you are, you can do this in the administrative area. It will take you two minutes and could save you a client. Even more importantly, it could keep someone from breaking into your website and updating some of your links to point to malicious software rather than your tools.

The other thing I want you to think about is your CRM. What could a hacker get to if he got to your CRM? All your client lists, right? He'd be able to email your clients as you, right? Most CRMs are set up specifically to blast emails to lists of people. What if an attacker sent a message to all of your clients as you and told them to do something like load a file or go to a website? Would they do it? Enable 2FA on your CRM.

Just one other quick comment, - multifactor authentication that's pointed to your email might not be good enough. I've seen a lot of options out there that allow you to turn on MFA and point it to your email. It sends you an email to confirm that you are who you say you are.

But here's the catch, if an attacker gets access to your e-mail—which, if you have 2FA enabled, is pretty difficult to do, but still - then he can go into things like your website or your accounting software or anything that sends 2FA to your email. If you change your password using the "password reset" button, that also goes to your email, and a hacker can gain access to that additional component. This is a popular way for an attacker to spread laterally.

I recommend that if you set up MFA to point to email, make sure the attacker can't go in and reset your password using that email account.

Back Up Everything

Question: Do you tell your clients to back up their servers and their domain controllers?

Of course. You tell them that they need to have these backups in place. But are they in place for you as well? What about backing up your website? And backing up your documentation? How about your CRM? All of these cloud-based services can be backed up. Now, I know, you are thinking they are already backed up by the cloud-provider. What if they have an outage? What if something goes wrong and they cannot get your data back? Do you want to be dependent on that?

Evaluate Your DNS

What are you leaking when it comes to DNS? What is open out there? What do people have access to? What DNS entries are hanging out there for anybody to see?

One thing you can do is remove any text records you use as part of a migration. For example, let's say you migrated to Microsoft 365 from an on-prem Exchange server. Maybe you used a service to help that migration go smoothly. Did you have to create a text record to help with the transition? Maybe to identify yourself as the owner of the domain. Delete all these records, because you don't want them accessible to anyone who can figure what accounts you might have created for that transition, or how to phish your users based on tools they are used to seeing.

How can you do this? Check this out: go to DNSDumpster.com. Enter your domain name. It will give you a list of DNS entries that are hanging around out there. You might want to port-scan the places that pop up and make sure they are good and locked down. Trust me, if you are not checking, other people are...

Learn What to Put on your Website and What Not to Put on Your Website

Don't publish your tools.

For example, if you publish a portal login on your site, and an attacker gets access to your website, he could point in this portal, log in somewhere else, harvest the credentials, and get in. Even if this isn't the location your team uses to log in, think about the type of mischief a hacker could create by figuring out the names, email addresses and passwords of some of your clients. They could call into your help desk with this information and make all kinds of trouble for you and your clients.

The other thing I've seen a lot of MSPs out there do is publish remote support tools right on their website. If an attacker gets access to your site and points those tools to his own tools, your clients might end up connecting and rolling out the red carpet to these bad guys. I would strongly suggest that you not put links to your tools on your website. You could have an easy to type in URL like help.yourcompany.com that would allow your client to connect, and you wouldn't have to worry about your website becoming an attack vector.

Prevent Brute-Force Attacks

Let's take a look at two different websites to help understand why preventing brute-force attacks is so important.

How would you figure out brute-force attacks are being prevented? One easy way would be to fish around until you find the link to their administrative interface. Now that you have access to the login page for the administrative interface, what could you do? How about enter a user name and password and see what happens. If there's a system set up to prevent brute force attacks you might get an alert telling you that you only have so many more tries before the account is locked or your source IP address is blocked. The other option would be after you try a couple of passwords and you cannot access the administrative page anymore. There is a third option. Nothing happens and you keep trying new usernames and passwords.

You want your site to show a password attempt count down or block the source IP address after a few tries. Why is this important? If you're hardening your website, if you're taking the right steps, you want to advertise it.

There are two reasons for this. Obviously, you want to prevent a hacker from gaining access by trying different passwords over and over and over. On the other hand, if clients or prospects were to stumble across the administrative interface for your website, they would know that there's some sort of brute force technology in place. In short, you want to present a secure posture.

Audit Your Certificates

The next thing I want you to do is audit your certificates.

When auditing MSPs, sometimes we find that their websites don't have that little padlock—that I'm-secure symbol—at the far left of the browser's URL field. If your site doesn't have this, you're sending a signal to your prospective clients that you don't have your ducks in a row when it comes to security.

What do you do to keep this from happening? First, check to see when your certificates expire. Document this somewhere that will alert you when they are coming up for expiration. If they're set to expire within a month, replace them right away. Do not wait. I also suggest you do this for your clients, too, because when a website certificate, or any certificate, expires, they'll get notices saying that things are insecure. This obviously undermines your authority as a security expert who has all of your ducks in a row.

Okay, you will want to do this for all of your certificates, not just the one for your website. That means a lot of hunting. Fortunately, Google has put together a way for folks to do this. Go to: TransparencyReport. Google.com/https/Certificates.

Type in your domain, then click "include subdomains." When the search results come up, you'll see tons of sites. You may see certificates that are long since gone. Make sure they in fact, don't still exist. Then make sure you don't have any old file servers or other services out there that still have open access. This is a good time to double-check everything to ensure that you don't have anything out there you don't want accessible to the outside world.

Polish Your Business Facade

The next thing I want you to do is look at the front of your business.

If your business had a brick-and-mortar storefront, if it were sitting on Main Street, what would it look like to someone driving by or walking by? Would it look inviting? Would it look like something you would want to go in and check out?

Start by googling yourself. This is what a prospective client is going to do, right? Google yourself personally, then google your business, and follow all the links that come up. Do you have a bad reviews? What else is showing up out there when someone searches for you?

Then go to news.google.com and create alerts for your company name and website. If something comes up and it's about you, and it's in the news, you might want to know about it. I'd also add an alert for your name and some of your favorite clients.

What about other things you're leaking? I mean, not just on the regular web. But what else do you have when it comes to an attack surface? There's an extremely extensive search engine called Shodan. io. Use that to dig in and see what you have out on the Internet of things. You'll need to learn the lingo and the commands in order to use Shodan, but it's worth your time. I've used it to find cameras, phone systems, and other devices that were long since forgotten on some of our target networks.

Finally, have you claimed your Facebook presence? Have you claimed your Google Local presence? If not, you want to claim these right away and confirm that they're yours, because the last thing you want is somebody else claiming them. Here's the list I would make sure to claim: Facebook, LinkedIn, Instagram, Twitter, Google My Business, TikTok, and YouTube. Maybe Yelp too.

People tell me all the time, "I don't want to mess with social networking. I'm not even going to sign up for a Facebook account because I don't want to deal with it." But as a CEO, or an engineer at an IT company, you must grab your social networking presence before someone else does. You don't want to be in a situation where somebody impersonates you by creating a false page and then uses it to reach out to your social network. Don't have stuff on your pages that you wouldn't want potential clients to see. When you are setting up these accounts, use incorrect birth dates and refrain from putting extensive personal data on the site.

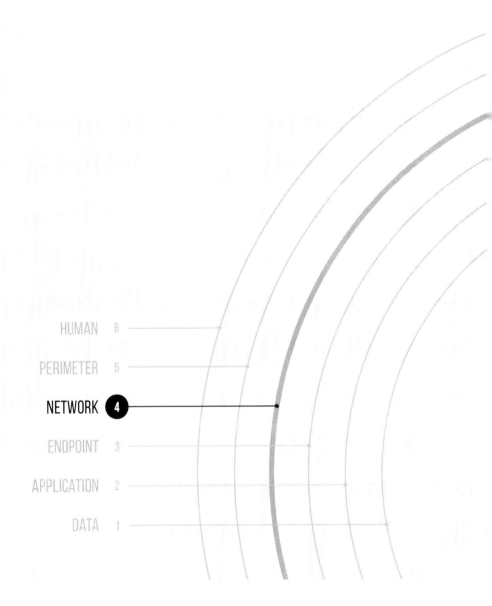

HUMAN 6

PERIMETER 5

NETWORK **4**

ENDPOINT 3

APPLICATION 2

DATA 1

NETWORK

Once hackers get in—and there are many ways to bypass a perimeter—the best way to defend yourself is to isolate their opportunities. If your network remains wide open and you're not reducing user rights to only what they need to do their job, you're making it easy for a hacker to do some serious damage.

CHAPTER 10
ACTIVE DIRECTORY HARDENING

About a year ago, we got a call from an MSP
whose largest client got infected with ransomware
and they had to pay the ransom.

The ransom started at $500,000. The client had cyber insurance and the insurance company negotiated with the attackers. Did you know that there are people who specialize in negotiating ransom payments down? Well there are, and if you ever experience an event like this you are going to want to engage them. When all was said and done, the ransom ware reduced to $140,000. Still, that's a lot of money for a couple of hackers to walk away with, right?

I want to spend some time on why the client had to pay the ransom. Then I want to ask some questions, such as whether an audit could have helped. And I want to help you understand how to prevent something like this from happening on your watch.

According to the forensics team, the attackers gained access to the network on August 8, but they didn't deploy ransomware immediately. In fact, they didn't deploy the ransomware until October 23. Think about that: months passed between the day when the attackers gained access and the day when they actually went to work.

You might be thinking, "Why? Why this gap? Why let so much time go by between August 8 and October 23?" The answer is—and we're seeing this in other organizations, too—that the attackers have an automated process that tries to exploit various vulnerabilities and access networks. They use the same type of process with phishing. You could think of it like a bunch of little robots that are trying to gain access to networks.

Once they gain access there are two manual steps to the process of deploying ransomware. The first is pretty obvious. The attackers want to manually enumerate the environment to see what they've got. Why do they need to know what they have access to? They want to see what kind of ransom they'll be able to charge. They may also have data that they can exfiltrate and sell back to the victim or sell to someone else.

The second step is a little bit trickier. They want to destroy the backups. Hackers are much more successful at getting paid when the victim cannot restore their backups and get back up and running. Destroying backups is a pretty big task and the attacker can't just depend on automation for that. You have to find backups and kill them.

With all this manual labor, ransomware attacks are much like projects. The hackers have a backlog, just as most of us do when it comes to project work.

There are two problems here for MSPs: how do you prevent the attacker from getting in, and how do you find them if they got in. How did the attacker get in? According to forensics folks, the attackers got in through RDP. Let me repeat that. The attackers got in through RDP that was opened to the outside world. As all your engineers know, this is a bad idea, but it still gets missed all the time. I just did a search on shodan.io and there are 4,535,567 RDP ports open to the outside world right now. So we aren't doing great on the first problem: keeping the attackers from getting in.

The next problem is that most of us aren't looking for the activity that takes place when the attackers get in. Read on.

What the Hackers Did

This event was a bit of a convoluted situation. What happened was that the CFO needed access from her iPad, which was equipped with a VPN-access-capable agent, to her computer. One of the engineers at the MSP got the CFO to access her computer through the iPad's built-in VPN. While setting it up, the engineer put a forwarding rule in for RDP from the outside world. He disabled it after he was able to get her up and running and went about his business. The CFO had an issue connecting one evening a few weeks later. She called the service desk, frustrated because she had work to do. The service desk logged into the firewall, saw the disabled firewall rule and enabled it. The CFO was back up and running, and the ticket was closed on the first call.

When RDP gets published to the outside world, attackers start working on brute-forcing it immediately. In this case, after a few hours of being published to the outside world, they found an account they were able to access the machine with. The user account had low privileges, so they weren't able to do much. Within minutes they escalated their privileges to that of a local administrator. This gave them enough rights to do something called pass the hash (see chapter 11), where they used a program called Mimi Katz to dump the LSASS service. Then they took the results from this dump file and used it to get to another computer that's in the environment where one of their local IT resources was logged in. This local IT resource had domain admin rights.

The attackers used the same tactic on the local IT resource's account. With domain administrative rights, the attackers were able to move to any computer on the network.

The next thing attackers do is hunt for backups. In this case, they were successful. They discovered the MSP's backup storage inside the environment. The backup storage was joined to the domain, which means that if you have domain admin rights, you can get to it and delete the backups. So they deleted all the backups before they deployed the ransomware.

What You Can Do

First and foremost, don't publish RDP to the outside world. Don't even set up a rule in a firewall for testing, you never know who might come by troubleshooting something and "fix it" by enabling the rule you set up.

Next, make sure you don't have a local admin account that uses the same password on all the machines inside your environment. Each device having the same local password allowed the attackers to easily move from one computer to the next.

If you have local IT resources, make sure they do not use the account with domain administrative rights to login to their computer for daily use. The hackers used the pass-the-hash technique to get to a machine where a guy who has domain admin credentials is logged in. On this topic, never leave an account logged in as a domain administrator. Even though the IT resource might have locked his computer and left for the weekend, he's still logged in to his domain admin account. If hackers can get onto that machine they will quickly have domain admin privileges.

After the hackers got to the backups, they encrypted the hypervisor. One thing to think about: the attackers want to have the ability to restore everything. They want everything to come back online after you pay the ransom. When you're protecting your clients, make sure that your hypervisor is also not part of Active Directory. That may mean you have to set up a secondary domain just for your hypervisors. I know, this sounds like a ton of work but which would you rather do? Spend weeks rebuilding after an attacker walks right through your network or set up a secondary domain?

In addition, the MSP had the RMM installed on the backup storage. The reason I'm bringing that up is because some of you have access to backup servers and storage servers that are hosting backups inside your RMMs. If you do, and if attackers get into your RMM, they could deploy ransomware to all of your backups and your servers with one script. They would be able to deploy ransomware not only to all your client devices but also to your backups without too much effort. Put your backups on a separate management network with a separate RMM. Think of a red forest completely on its own.

In the end, the insurance company paid for the recovery. It paid for everything, including the forensics. Everything had to be rebuilt. But this is where things got a little crazy.

The victim asked for a third-party assessment. And if, as an MSP, you're not offering third-party auditing as part of your services, your client will be forced to seek it elsewhere—in the ransomware case, the client went to another MSP for that assessment. If having a third-party do some of these assessments for you isn't already part of your QBR, it should be.

It will prevent somebody less qualified than you from evaluating your work. Somebody who may have a different intention than protecting your client. Someone who is interested in taking your client.

I have some numbers to share with you. According to an annual data breach report, 87 percent of breaches take months to get noticed. The good news: that gives you time. Once the attackers get in with their automated process, it takes a while for them to engage and start executing their attack. If you can notice the breach, you can prevent exfiltration and ransomware.

That data breach report also pointed out that 84 percent of victims had evidence in their logs that the breach was happening. The bad news: most of the MSPs we evaluate don't have auditing set up inside their logs. Most of the time the event logs are overwriting themselves, or the MSPs don't have the correct audit events turned on to begin with.

In the case of this ransomware event, there was no alert for failed log-in attempts. The only thing the attackers did was escalate privileges, and in order to do that they had to update the admin group membership. That too should have triggered an alarm or an alert.

You're probably thinking, "Doesn't Active Directory take care of this stuff for me? Don't we already have all that Active Directory stuff in place?"

No. In fact, when you set up a server, it has just a bare-minimum audit policy configured. Why? Because logs take up space, and Microsoft doesn't want to blow its servers up by filling them with audit logs and event entries. It wants you to set up for the most common use of its server, which is file storage.

Let's talk about how to set up audit logs. The default is to overwrite the audit logs as needed. And you may want to set a retention period inside those audit logs. (By the way, this is not a soup-starter kit for setting up all your auditing inside Active Directory. This is just about setting up the audit logs themselves.) Microsoft has an advanced audit security policy component with about nine major options. To get to advanced audit policy, simply bring up your group policy settings, go into security settings, and then go into the advanced security audit policy configuration.

There is plenty of documentation out there on what to set up for your advanced security audit policy. You can find best practices for workstations, servers, Active Directory controllers, and so on. Just a reminder: "Your mileage will vary." I don't want you to do this across the board to all your servers without testing, because if you do, you're going to create a lot of noise. You will end up getting a bunch of logs and tons of alerts. Your team will be overwhelmed, and they won't have enough time to respond or fix anything. I want you to avoid that. Set it up on one or two server types first, slowly adding to the devices you are performing this level of analysis on.

For a comprehensive guide to setting up your advanced security audit policies, visit **GalacticScan.com/Active-Directory**

CHAPTER 11
PREVENTING LATERAL MOVEMENT

Imagine it's four o'clock on a Saturday morning.
You just got a call from the security operations center,
and one of your favorite clients has something weird
going on in its environment.

All your client's servers stopped checking in around twenty minutes before
the security operations center called. The team was able to get to the
routers and the firewalls. They weren't able to log into any of the servers.

If you're in that situation, what do you do next?

You'd pull yourself out of bed, log in to your laptop and look.
Is there anything bad showing up in the logs? Looks good.
Just no servers able to check in.

You reach out to your primary contact. You say, "Hey, I just want to let
you know that this is going on." and you coordinate meeting up in the
parking lot. You decide to meet at 8:00 a.m. Does this sound familiar?

You go back to bed, roll around for a little bit. You try to get some sleep,
and, well, it doesn't really work out, so you get up and get some work
done. Then you get in your car and drive over there, and you're thinking,
"Gosh, I wonder what's going on. Did the server room overheat? Did
a breaker pop cutting power and turn everything off and the backup
battery is running without properly shutting down the network?"

You meet your primary contact. He opens the door to the building
for you, and you walk in. The first computer you see says "Cannot
connect to the server" on the screen. You kind of expect that, right?
Because if all the servers and the environment are offline, that DHCP
is offline to be able to get on there. There will be a lot of reasons for
something like this to happen.

After the client finally gets you logged in and on the machine, you see something like this:

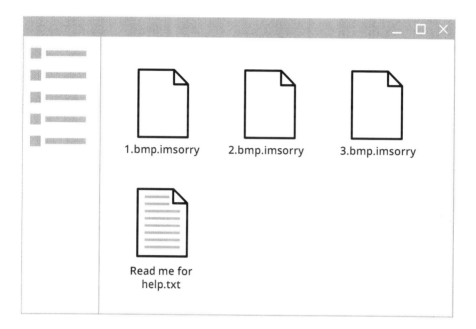

1.bmp.imsorry   2.bmp.imsorry   3.bmp.imsorry

Read me for
help.txt

This is your first indication that it's not just the servers that are offline. This is your first indication that you have something else going on. The entire environment was affected, both servers and workstations.

Every workstation was ransomed—same with the servers. Think about this.

There are a couple of things you need to do right away. First, check your backups. You might find the local backups destroyed. However, there was a cloud-based backup solution in place. If you don't have cloud-based backups, get them, and make sure they're not sharing any credentials and are in no way related to the local backups that you're using as a quick restore point.

Let's say the client had cyber insurance and wanted to get the insurance company engaged. Then the insurance company said it wanted forensics to be taken care of and tells you not to touch anything. This is standard procedure: the insurance company will tell you (the MSP) to stand down, then get somebody in forensics to review the network data (this will take time!).

The following are some questions I want you to ask yourself in situations like this.

The first one is: **When can I start the recovery?**

If forensics will be involved, you won't be able to touch anything until they're done. In the case described above, it will take at least seven days before the client is able to get started on some of the devices.

The next question is: **How long will my client be down?**

Your client will ask you that question.
And you may want to have some answers ready.

One thing you might consider is having some loaner server hardware that you can bring online. You can spin up your client's environment on loaner hardware. That's one of the things we used to do—I always had some way to get the client back up and running without having to revert to the original hardware. If workstations are part of the investigation, you have to figure out how to deal with that, too.

The next question is: **Does my client have to pay the ransom or not?**

We want our partners to draw up a data asset list with their clients. Keep this list in a spot that's easily accessible. That way you can figure out if you have backups of every single thing your client will need in order to get back online. You will also want to indicate what the priority is for bringing that data online.

Another question is: **Am I going to be liable?**

You won't know the answer to that question for a while. A partner brought us in around three months after an event like this happened because they needed somebody to help rebuild the client's trust in them. They still don't know if they are going to be fighting with the client's insurance company over liability.

I suggest you focus on the first three questions and make whoever provides your errors and omissions insurance aware of the problem. If you don't have an errors and omissions policy, you might want to look into it. (See chapter 5, "Cyber Liability Insurance" for more information.)

So how do we prevent this?

The answer involves three things: local accounts, domain users and domain admins. All those pieces play into an event like the one I described above.

I know some of you are thinking, "This doesn't really matter, because I have a SIEM," or "This doesn't really matter, because I invested in an MDR." Here's the thing: if you get prevention right, and somebody attacks your environment, you're not so dependent on your defenses. You've got good, solid walls protecting you. If your defenses are a little off, or maybe if somebody is asleep at the wheel for a minute, then you won't have to go through what I just described.

So think about the layered approach to security:
What do you have in place at each of these layers?

I'm going to assume that the human layer was bypassed. I'm going to assume that the perimeter layer was bypassed. And I'm going to assume that you, like most MSPs, have a very flat network inside this environment that has all the workstations on the same wire as the servers and that you don't have VLANs or trust separations inside the network.

Now think about what you would want to do if you were trying to get in. Instead of being the MSP—the defender—I want you to put on your hacker hat, or maybe your hacker hoodie, and think like a hacker for a minute. How do you get in?

The answer is probably phishing, right? This never fails and always gets you access to at least one computer inside the network. It doesn't matter how much training users receive—they will still click a link if there's enough emotion, if there's enough urgency. With a little bit of social engineering and a link that seems believable the users are going to click it and let the attacker in.

When you phish your way in, you probably won't end up on the computer in Human Resources, which would have a bunch of fun stuff on it like personally identifiable information, access to payroll, or even a company employee list with emergency contacts. You could end up on someone in IT's computer, but chances are you'll end up on Mary's computer. You see, Mary is the receptionist. She's super busy. She's taking calls. She's interrupted often. She's always in a hurry to help other people around the office.

She's the most susceptible to phishing. The people who are the busiest, the people who are the hardest for you to get in front of, the people who can't hold still long enough to go through phishing training —those are the ones who are usually the most susceptible.

So what can you do next?

If you're an attacker, when you get onto this system, the first thing that's going to happen is you're going to sit in a queue. It will be a little while before you get to this new find. Why? Because you're busy. I mean, you've got all these other victims and all these other opportunities to explore. You may not get to Mary's computer for a little while. Some people ask me how long the queue is now. I've heard folks in the MDR community say two or three weeks, which gives you some time to take advantage of the knowledge that somebody's there. You have a little time to figure out that someone is present.

But as the hacker, after you get through the ransomware queue, you want to establish persistence. This means inserting something into the scheduler, maybe putting something into the registry. It's a way of making sure you can get back onto that device.

What's the next thing you're going to do as a hacker?

You figure out what the heck you have. You scan the computer and look for treasure—for personally identifiable information, passwords, tokens, credit card numbers, or gold coins (okay, just seeing if you are paying attention with the gold coin comment). You're on Mary's computer, and she's a receptionist, so maybe you won't get a whole lot.

Then you look around and see what else is out there, maybe do a port scan. This is a big, risky step. If you scan the network and you are noisy about it, the folks watching the network might notice you. You will want to take it slow. This would be like walking from room to room with a flashlight while robbing a house versus turning on all the lights at once.

While you're doing that, you look at the device itself to see who else has local administrative rights. That's a pretty easy command. You could just do that right on the command line. You type "net user" into your shell and hit enter. That's not going to set off any alarms, and it'll tell you whether this user is a local user and which other admins, local admins, are on the device. Sometimes MSPs spend a lot of time coming up with really fancy naming conventions for the admin accounts—I've seen everything from completely randomized springs to superheroes. If you're doing that, you're wasting your time, because hackers can figure out with a simple command line who has a local admin on the device.

The next thing you do as a hacker is figure out if there's a way to move —get from Mary's machine to the next one. Most of the time, you can.

When we perform assessments of MSPs we see three different types of accounts that could be used for this. There's usually a local admin back-door account. We also see local admin image accounts. Finally, we see domain admin accounts. Often we see these accounts with shared passwords. These passwords are often shared, either across the entire MSP or the entire environment. Sometimes the MSP only passwords shared among individual locations and among individual clients. These are all risky behaviors because they allow an attacker to move from computer to computer.

Another type of shared credential we find is shared user passwords. Let's say Mary logs on to her computer as staff, and the staff user also logs into five other computers. Now that password could be used to log on to those other five computers as well. As an attacker you would be very happy to find a shared user account because you can use it to move to other computers.

Why do people use shared passwords on computers? They believe they're safe just because they've created a really strong password. They have a local admin account for a back-door account, and it requires a thirty-two-character password. They've done all the right steps to create a strong password. It has punctuation, uppercase letters, lowercase letters, and even some numbers.
The problem: it's the same on every computer.

Even if you're all sharing a password , though, you're not safe from lateral movement. The attacker doesn't have to crack the password to use it. That's because of this fancy thing called pass the hash (see chapter 12).

So as an MSP, what can you do?

First, Microsoft has this thing called LAPS. But if you're running in a big MSP, if you're planning on growing your organization, LAPS doesn't scale very well. You have to set it up on each domain you support, and for the clients that don't have a domain, you are out of luck. Then when you need the password, you have to log into the domain controller in order to get it. Imagine having to do that for every one of your clients when they have a ticket that requires you to work on something that requires administrative credentials.

You're probably thinking, "Oh, my gosh, that won't be easy." But it's not too difficult, and here's why: you're going to store those passwords in your RMM or password manager. On the RMM side, simply establish a special user-created field. If you are thinking about storing it in your password manager, be careful where you put your API key. There are a few scripts floating around out there that store the API key in the script itself. Well, that would give an attacker access to your API, and thus all the passwords in your password manager if they get access to the script. How do they get access to the script? Often when scripts are run through your RMM they are downloaded to the computer.

You also might be thinking, "I don't want to store them in the RMM because somebody might get into it." But if hackers get to your RMM and see passwords, they could just run any script they want to and change them. If they get that far in, and they're able to see those user-defined fields and those passwords, they can do whatever the heck they want.

I want you to script this password change. I don't want you to just manually change these passwords. Why not? Because at some point, some of your people will win the lottery. It may not be the kind of lottery that allows them to move to Hawaii. But it might be the kind of lottery that gets them a brand-new job, and they're going to leave your company. So you want to have a script you can run to change all these passwords quickly for all of your clients' computers.

There's one more thing you should consider.
First, a question: can you use a domain user to move laterally?

The answer is yes. We're seeing domain user security groups stuffed in the local admin group on all the computers in some networks. Heck, I've even seen the domain user security group added to the domain administrator group. How do you fix this or walk it back? It is going to start with a lot of user education. Some of you swear you would never do anything like that, but let's say you just won a new client. You are setting them up on your standards. You're not going to look at the settings on this new client's workstations, are you? Are you going to go through and checkout all the members of their domain administrator group? If you don't, it's difficult to notice.

To prevent this problem, you are going to need to audit your environments, and set up users so that they don't have local admin rights. That's a big ask, I know. Trust me, it is worth the effort.

Another problem we often see is that domain admins are logged in to computers. Why is this a big deal?

Put on your hacker hat again. If you can get to a machine where a domain admin is logged in, you might not be able to get the credentials from the NTLM hash, but you can get them in a different way.

Basically, you can dump the LSASS service, and then, again using that Mimi Katz solution, use the pass-the-hash technique to move laterally with the domain admin credentials.

I would even create an alert to let you know if you have a domain admin logged in to a machine that's been idle for more than an hour. You could create a script to log the domain administrator off the machine automatically, or maybe create a ticket so you can follow up with your engineers. Ask them, "Why are you leaving yourselves logged in?"

Furthermore, don't give normal users domain admin rights. I know. You have to. They need to log in and, do updates for some crazy piece of software. You can't figure out how to make it work any other way. I am here to tell you there are better solutions out there. You could use some software that only gives them these rights when they are applying updates. You could just give them local admin access to the devices that they have to update. Also, consider giving them these rights using a separate account than the one they use to log in on a daily basis.

This is critical: do not log in to workstations with your domain admin accounts.

Let me repeat that, because I want everybody to understand it. If this were third grade, I'd tell you to write it down. Ten times. Because I've audited your networks. I know this is happening. Do not log in to workstations with your domain admin accounts. You don't know where those computers have been or what users have gotten into on them. If you log in as a domain administrator, you're running the risk of giving up your domain admin rights to an attacker. Instead, use the local admin account that you just created by script so that you never have to worry about giving up your domain admin rights.

Finally, never, ever, ever log in to your backup servers or your backup solution from the servers you are backing up. I know this is one of those cases where you might think, "I'm in a hurry. I can just open a web browser and pop over there." But browser passwords get cached even if you don't want them to. That becomes an attack vector along which someone can move in and destroy those backups.

Remember, ransomware doesn't work if it doesn't kill the backups. Attackers are very interested in killing these backups, and you are very interested in protecting them.

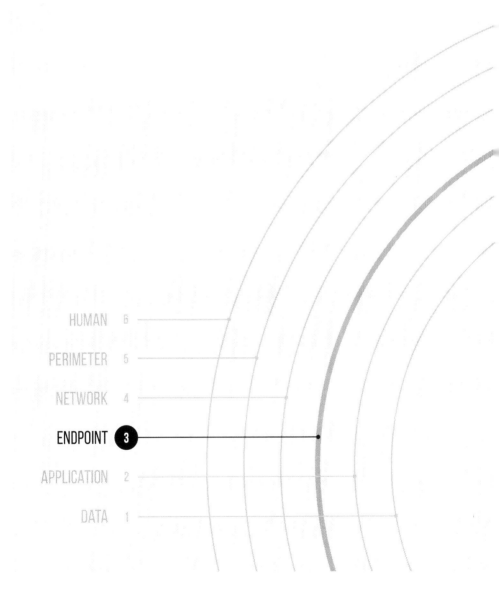

HUMAN 6

PERIMETER 5

NETWORK 4

ENDPOINT 3

APPLICATION 2

DATA 1

ENDPOINT

Endpoint security is probably the area in your cyber stack where you are most likely to overinvest and create overlap with some components, while underinvesting and leaving holes in others. Endpoint security has been around for decades, but it's now one of the most critical components of your cyber stack, especially as we move beyond the confines of the conventional workplace. Identifying endpoint components to secure and developing ways to mitigate attacks are essential. And securing your cloud-based endpoints is equally as important as securing your local endpoints, if not more so.

CHAPTER 12
BYPASSING ANTIVIRUS

I want to devote an entire chapter to bypassing antivirus software because many businesses rely too heavily on their perimeters for defense.

Many simply rely on firewalls to address this. Today, frankly, that's not an effective golden bullet because we're in a work-from-everywhere culture.

For better or for worse, antivirus remains a vital part of your organization's critical security layers—despite the fact that in nearly half the instances in which a company suffers a data breach, the attackers simply bypassed the antivirus systems. They basically bypassed the stuff that was in place to protect the endpoints.

Why on earth is this still happening? To figure it out, we need to take a quick trip down memory lane, back to a time when hackers were up to something other than making money—when hackers were kind of funny and trying to do new things.

It was August of 2003 when the Blaster worm shuffled across the internet. It had one simple message, directed at Bill Gates: stop making money and start fixing your software. And that was it. Wouldn't it be nice if that was all we were dealing with today?

But before that, in May of 2000, the ILOVEYOU virus came along—an awesome virus. This is when viruses started to go haywire, and everything started to go sideways. If you remember, it was just a little email love letter. If you clicked on the letter, it would immediately start doing stuff like destroying your files. It forced organizations to shut down their email systems for a week or so while the virus was cleaned out.

Can you imagine that today? Just saying, "Gosh, we have to turn off email for the next week until this virus goes away"? That's how companies were avoiding it! Think about how that would affect our day-to-day activities.

Here's how the virus worked. The user clicked on the love letter, then it went through the hard drive and randomly overwrote Office files, image files, and audio files. The next thing it did was copy itself to all the addresses in the user's address book and send out another message to everybody out there. Does that sound familiar?

That was the first real example of social engineering. And just think how brilliant it was: a love letter coming from somebody at the office or somebody you know—isn't that kind of provocative? It seemed so harmless, yet it was so destructive.

This is where most of the ransomware we work with today has its roots. And I bet you've seen ransomware that spreads the same way —social-engineering its way in, getting a script or a loader to work, then blasting ransomware across the network. The ILOVEYOU virus was the granddaddy of them all. It started all the crud that many of us are dealing with today.

The ILOVEYOU virus ended up costing the US economy $8.7 billion. However, you look at it, that's a huge number. The reason it was so expensive is because email systems got turned off. The other reason is because it took so much time to clean up the mess.

I remember when I started my MSP. One of our clients actually got the virus. This was before people had antivirus on their computers. A lot of you probably remember those days. You didn't put it on because it made things slower. Some people still shun it today. In fact, when we're doing analysis in the field, we find that around 10 percent of the engineers out there disable their antivirus because they feel like it makes things slower. It's looking over what they're doing.

The client that got hit by the virus was a cabinetry shop, of all things. The firm made custom cabinetry for kitchens, and it had this special computer that would cut all the countertops. That thing ran twenty-four hours a day, seven days a week. The staff was so afraid it would stop running that when the virus hit, it was a complete emergency. We had to run over there right away.

Here's the funny thing: only one person in that organization got the virus or was even susceptible to it. Why? Because only one person in the entire company used e-mail.

There's a lot of misunderstanding out there when it comes to antivirus.

But before I correct these misunderstandings, I want to spend a minute talking about layers of security.

Indiana Jones and the Temple of Doom was my favorite movie when I was a kid. In this movie, Indiana Jones has to navigate through a tunnel that presents a variety of challenges, including spikes coming up from the floor. Of course, Indiana is a hero and overcomes everything the villains throw at him. But if every scene involved spikes coming up from the floor, it wouldn't be a very exciting movie, because you would know what's coming each time. And Indiana wouldn't be much of a hero if he had only one challenge to overcome. So I want you to think of your antivirus the same way.

Another example: Do you remember *Indiana Jones and the Last Crusade*? In that movie, Indiana has to make it through a number of layers of security, and they're all completely different. And after he solves some crazy riddles, he makes it to his final decision point, where choosing the correct chalice is a matter of life and death.

That's what your endpoint security needs to be—something that presents a new challenge at every turn. You want a security model that has six layers, but not homogenous layers like an onion's. The layers should be diverse, like the Indiana Jones challenges, which incorporate a riddle that you have to figure out at each step of the way.

What do I mean by this? When you're putting together your security solutions, you should use a different vendor and a different tool in each layer along the way to that final grail—the assets you're protecting. Impose a challenge at every step, because if you don't, you'll end up with a gap that allows an attacker to gain a foothold.

Endpoint security now includes a variety of protections: USB lockdown, signature antivirus, heuristic antivirus, application whitelisting, active threat detection, TPM chips. This is all stuff that's living in the endpoint layer. So how does antivirus detect and block known viruses?

Signature-based antivirus, does exactly what it sounds like. It uses a signature that contains details about the attackers. It knows maybe a little piece of the virus file, or it has a hash of that file, or it looks for strings and functions that match known malicious software. It's really good at finding something like the ILOVEYOU virus, because that virus was just a VBScript. It was simple. It always looked the same. If you had a signature back then that was looking for any one of the functions in the ILOVEYOU virus, you'd have an easy job blocking it.

You have this virus database that gets updated and pushed out to clients. This is one of the reasons it's so important to have alerting, especially with signature-based antivirus—to make sure your agents are checking back in with your antivirus solution.

Let's say you're an attacker and you know your target uses signature-based antivirus. How will you get around it? (Why am I telling you how to break in? Because if you understand how to break in, then you understand why the security is in place and what it's doing.)

You know that signature-based antivirus is only looking for the specific strings and functions it already recognizes. So the first thing you do is manually rename some of your code. If your code has a function or a variable that includes the word "payload," for example, it's going to alert the antivirus.

And if you're an MSP and use the word "payload" in a function, your antivirus won't be happy with you, especially if it's a macro. That's a pretty good indicator to the antivirus that hey, a naughty person is trying to get into your system right now. But if you're an attacker, you have a team of attackers reminding you to not use words like "payload."

There are tools hackers use to get around having to rewrite code completely. One is called a packer. It packs your code, usually by compressing the executable a bit, then it sets itself up to unpack the code with a known tool. It basically changes everything into a bunch of gobbledygook. An example is one called Amber; it's freely available on GitHub. Why is this all important?

If you're attacking somebody and want to see all the things that person is typing, you might decide to deploy a key logger. But if you just installed the keylogger without packing it first, antivirus would find it. Antivirus would recognize the functions and the calls that the code makes and quickly realize this is grabbing the text that someone is typing. A packer moves this code around and makes it really hard for antivirus to see what is happening under the hood.

Another tool hackers use is something called a crypter, which encases their code in an encrypted binary and sends it out. This is similar to a packer, but it adds obfuscation or encryption to the mix. The goal is the same as the packer – make the binary look different to avoid antivirus detection. These encryption methods can be as simple as an XOR with a unique key.

Hacker tools change all the time, and antivirus vendors are often not able to keep up. So hackers know it's really important to build their own code, because if they pack it or use a crypter they are still easily traced back to the original source. "Homemade" code is particularly effective because antivirus may never have seen it before.

Microsoft is aware of this, so it proposes a solution. Why don't we require all our software to be signed? Digital signatures—won't that solve the problem?

Here's the problem with digital signatures. If you were a hacker and were trying to get into a network, what would you do to get around a certificate requirement? You would socially engineer your way into having one. Using a fake website, you could simply buy a certificate.

How hard would it be to create a fake website? Not hard at all. You would just scrape the existing website of anyone standing up on a new domain— maybe a .net domain or maybe a .ca domain; it doesn't really matter. Just stand up a new domain, use a legitimate-sounding domain name, pick up a PO box and a burner phone, then get yourself a digital signature.

Today, more than 80 percent of viruses are signed. These viruses use legitimate certificates as well.

So the new mission is to adapt to a constantly changing virus threatscape. How do you stay ahead of it?

A heuristic approach is the solution everybody landed on, because we can't know what's going to be out there next week. We can't even know what's out there now, because there are so many things happening. So we created algorithms to predict malware events.

Heuristic-based antiviruses do a couple of things. They look for patterns, and they look for software that's carrying out suspicious activity. They do this in two phases. The first is the pre-execution phase, in which the program looks at code fragments, hashes, and maybe even the entire code to figure out what's going on. The antivirus could even pull file properties as a reliable way to identify malicious software. Does that sound familiar?

It should. That's how signature-based antivirus works. Heuristic antivirus starts out like signature antivirus. In the pre-execution phase it takes similar steps. The main difference, however, is that heuristic antivirus uses an AI in the background—an artificial intelligence engine we'll call machine learning. Machine learning, rather than a person maintaining a database, is what identifies the naughty bits.

Now, we have a robot, which means more work for our code packers and crypters. Instead of creating a single executable using a code packer, an attacker might have to devise a tool that always creates a new executable. Hackers automated this stuff. They invented polymorphic code, which mutates every time it copies itself to a new location or server. If a user clicks on a link, it morphs the code every time the data is sent to a new victim. Now we're talking, right?

That's how hackers get past the pre-execution phase of heuristic antivirus.

In post-execution, one of the ways to analyze the behavior or events caused by hacker activity is something called sandboxing, in which the antivirus watches what the virus does inside a sandbox. And if the virus does something naughty, the antivirus stops it. But because that takes a lot of resources, it makes users unhappy. They start disabling stuff, and this leads to less security than we had before.

Machine learning isn't 100 percent accurate. If it were, we'd all be done with security. We'd all be sitting back, having margaritas at the beach. Back to reality. Machine learning has some weaknesses, and that's what the attackers go for. The first weakness is very simple: machine learning doesn't understand the implications of the model it creates. Sometimes machine learning stops patches or blows up computers if it identifies a ransomware target that isn't really ransomware. This ends up causing large-scale outages.

If the cure is worse than the disease, that's a major weakness.

The other weakness is that machine learning requires huge data sets, and it learns only if it's working with very clean data sets to generate its predictions. When we talk about learning, we're talking about a cycle much like the one used to teach a person a new skill. You start with training. Antivirus creators feed the antivirus both benign executables and malicious executables, then train it to predict which code will be malicious through multiple learning cycles. Once it has that predictive model, the antivirus goes into the production phase. There, it sees an unknown executable, processes it by that predictive model, and decides whether it's malicious or benign.

That's exactly how machine learning works. The issue is that the marketing of these products leads us to believe that something else is happening—that the tool is learning as it's running on our computers and that it's protecting us at the same time. But that's not what we're seeing in our labs and in our tests. We're seeing a model that looks more like an on and off switch. Learning and responding.

How does this virus behave? That's the big question.

The first thing you might look at is code injection: What processes does the virus attempt to push code into? Does it try to push code into known processes such as winlogin.exe, LSASS.exe, or servicehost? And why would it push something into winlogin.exe? That last question is where machine learning starts to fall apart. That's when you have a person making decisions.

Winlogin.exe is the process that manages the typing in of a password and username on the keyboard. It runs on all computers, and if you insert a keylogger into it, you can get users' passwords when they log in. They control or delete the login.

But the only way to insert a keylogger is to escalate privileges on the computer and move from the user space to the kernel space in the processor. As soon as you start seeing that type of behavior, that type of movement, and that type of escalation of privileges through code injection, you know you've got somebody doing something naughty.

Heuristic antivirus also looks for persistence. How do hackers create persistence on a computer? The easy way is to drop something into the startup folder. Obviously, if somebody's writing to the startup folder, or maybe adding things to the scheduler, you need to investigate.

But what about the registry? Of course, a hacker can add something to the registry, and that would also indicate that something bad is going on, but a lot of processes write in the registry. In fact, all these indicators could point to a process that's up to something malicious or a process that's engaging in its normal daily activity.

That's where machine learning comes in, because humans can't keep up with all the decisions that viruses are making. For example, some heuristic-based antiviruses look at network traffic and determine what the virus is trying to connect to in the outside world. Is it connecting with a known IP address? Or a bad IP address? How often is it sending traffic out? What patterns are in this traffic? Is it sending out Social Security numbers and credit card numbers? Or is it just sending a heartbeat? And what does that mean? Are commands coming through? What does that look like?

In addition, what does the virus look at? What files does it touch? What data is it pulling out of them? What's making it into memory? How quickly is it reading files? What files are modified? How many files are processing? How many files is it writing to? How many files is it writing to in a certain amount of time? What types of files are they? Where are the files located? Is the virus changing? Is it changing in entropy?

These are the things heuristic antivirus is looking for in the post-execution phase. But the antivirus can't look at everything all the time. At some point, it has to trust you.

How does a hacker get past this heuristic antivirus? This is where a stager (sometimes called a loader or a dropper) comes in.

What is a stager?

A stager sends your victim a link. He clicks the link, which might contain a macro or a bit of code. The link isn't the virus itself: it's just a very small executable or a script that enumerates the computer. Once it enumerates the computer, it determines what the next steps should be—how to access the real payload. It usually uses an encrypted backchannel, maybe over DNS, to avoid network protection.

In other words, instead of sending an HTTPS response over SSL, which a lot of our perimeter devices can detect, decrypt, and read, it goes through an encrypted backchannel. A backchannel is a channel that people aren't looking for Here's an example: a hacker creates a text record and sends the request over as the hostname, perhaps a long hostname. Then the DNS server gets a hostname response—a TXT record, which is the response to whatever the tool is asking for. In this case, it might be an executable. The stager enumerates the system, figures out what antivirus is there, then identifies what the weaknesses are in that particular antivirus. Then it executes a request, or an encrypted executable, on a backchannel to drop in and initiate the attack.

Let's say the victim is using SuperSecure antivirus. Like many other antivirus tools, SuperSecure can't scan everything. Even if it scanned every single file, it would never keep up. So SuperSecure doesn't check bitmaps or image files, MP4s—nothing big.

To bypass SuperSecure the stager simply requests a bitmap. The web server it's requesting from serves up the bitmap with the executable in it. When it gets down to the machine, the stager downloads the bitmap, then executes the code in memory without writing to disk. SuperSecure is none the wiser.

The bottom line: even if you're running a heuristics-based antivirus, make sure it's enabled and that it's getting updates. Think about how your antivirus provider gets its data and trains its AI engines. It's doing that with big data sets, much larger than the one you have in your organization. So you've got to get the updates for both heuristic and signature-based antivirus.

Next, make sure you're running alerts and that they are indicating whether antivirus is operating.

The endpoint comprises many layers. And hackers will always have a book of clues to help them penetrate those layers, just like the book Indy had when he was going through his adventures.

Your goal is to amass enough properly installed layers to protect you from these hackers. So here's a quick mission for you: What do you have going on in your endpoint layer? Think about what you have and how hackers can get around it. Because understanding what your defenses do and don't do is critical to keeping your clients safe. Spend twenty minutes on it. You don't have to provide more than one or two examples in order to get yourself thinking about the vulnerabilities within your security infrastructure.

If you're wondering whether your antivirus software is effective, visit **GalacticScan.com/Stack** to see if your solutions are working the way you expect.

CHAPTER 13
ENDPOINT SECURITY

Many organizations rely on their perimeter
defenses to protect their endpoints.

They use things like advanced firewalls to protect them from persistent threats directed at MSPs and their clients. But the perimeter is not viable as a castle wall and primary barrier in today's hybrid work environment. With your users finding themselves outside the corporate network, they are left depending on tools like antivirus. The problem? Hackers now just bypass antivirus software.

Why? Because hacking isn't about creating a neat little virus that you can brag about to your friends anymore. It's about the money—it's about making serious cash money.

To combat this, we've mainly landed on protecting the endpoints with antivirus. Starting with signature-based antiviruses. These were set up to scan for files. They looked for a very specific pattern of bits, and their job was simple: detect and block. They found the virus and stopped it from propagating and infecting machines.

This worked really great back in the day of the ILOVEYOU virus and viruses that didn't change over time. You could depend on an antivirus signature database to recognize and stop this type of threat. But signature-based antivirus was not able to tell you what the next file would look like. Hackers figured out how to address that, just change the way their executable looks.

Along comes a new breed of antivirus, that constantly adapts to changing threatscapes. It takes a heuristic approach, using algorithms and patterns not just to determine whether something is dangerous but also to *predict* whether something will be dangerous. It does this by operating in two different phases.

The first phase is the pre-execution phase. This is when the antivirus determines whether the bit or the code it detects does anything bad. Sound familiar? This is exactly how a typical signature-based antivirus works too. It uses code fragments and hashes and other pieces of information to create a reliable fingerprint, then it uses that fingerprint to determine whether the threat is a virus.

Hackers get around this with something called the polymorphic code. It's code that changes every time a user opens the file. It could even change when somebody downloads a new copy of the virus. When a victim clicks a link, the server gives the virus a completely new set of code. This is done through encryption. Hackers are basically repackaging the virus on the fly.

Now for phase two: the post-execution kicks in after the malware gets executed. If somebody clicks a link, the antivirus starts doing its thing. It tells you about the virus's behavior and what it touches and looks at. If the heuristics were working 100 percent of the time, we wouldn't have any issues getting it to detect malicious code. Once the malicious code is detected and shut down the endpoint would be safe. That isn't what we are seeing. In other words, we cannot expect an antivirus to completely protect us: if it could, we wouldn't need any other way to guard our endpoints.

I want to persuade you to change your mind-set around security layers. You need to create a maze of hurdles, that are difficult to guess and even harder to overcome. What does that mean? That means you have to use a variety of solutions, each in its own layer so it doesn't overlap with the others. And you have to use a different vendor for every step along the way.

Let's break that down.

First, as I said above, an attacker will probably make it by your antivirus, especially if it's a directed attack, and especially if he's focused on getting into your machine. But that doesn't mean you should avoid investing in an antivirus solution. Why? One of your top clients is hacked. The hackers get all the way through, and the client finds out that you didn't have antivirus installed on one of its computers. Just one. It doesn't even have to be one of the ones that was attacked. The client will submit an insurance claim. There will be a fast-talking insurance representative or a lawyer looking over your shoulder, and that guy is going to have a field day with your contract: "What do you mean you didn't have antivirus on one of these computers?"

I know that every single one of your contracts says you will install and maintain antivirus for your clients. But just from a risk-management standpoint, you need to have antivirus on *all* your clients' computers. If you don't, you're putting yourself in a really bad situation. You're putting yourself at risk of being run out of business. Folks coming after you in an event like this won't be super friendly.

Getting past antivirus, yes, that happens. But if you don't have antivirus in the first place, you'll be called negligent.

There are a couple of things you can do to prevent this. First, check to see that there are no mistakes in your antivirus implementation, especially when you're replacing one antivirus solution with another. One provider we audited had been moving from a signature-based antivirus to a heuristic-based antivirus, trying to do the right thing. This MSP even spent a little more for its new solution. But lo and behold, the installation missed around half the machines. You see, the script got through the first half of the machines, then it broke somehow and never installed on the rest. When we performed the assessment, we found a whole bunch of machines with missing antivirus.

Does your system check whether antivirus is installed? Does it alert you when the antivirus isn't running? Does it alert you when the antivirus needs updating? Your remote management tools can automatically perform those functions. But there are also things you can do manually to check whether your system is working as expected. How do you know your system is telling you the truth?

Here are a couple tips with antivirus: first, don't allow end users to disable the antivirus. In addition, make sure that viruses are reported back to you in some form of an alert. If you keep getting viruses on one particular machine, for example, arrange for it to trigger a ticket so you can investigate. You may want to trigger a ticket whenever a virus is found, but you certainly want to trigger a ticket when you see multiple events on a single machine. This is often an attacker trying to get past your defenses.

Also, if a hacker bypasses antivirus, make it really hard for him to move laterally through the network. Get him stuck in the mud.

Think about the COVID pandemic for a second. This virus wouldn't be very effective if it weren't so contagious. That's lateral movement from one person in the community to another. That's what we're trying to prevent when it comes to hacking. How do you do that?

First, understand how hackers move from point A to point B inside a network. One of the things they use is PowerShell. Why is PowerShell called PowerShell? Because it's super powerful, and it's a shell. Hackers love shells. Why? All you need is the command line, and you can get a lot of stuff done. You can get a lot of stuff done with a very small network connection. With PowerShell you can even encode your commands as you send them across the wire. This is helpful when the attacker is routing the command through a series of multiple computers.

You're probably thinking, "Bruce, why don't I just prevent the hacker from getting in in the first place?" Because at some point, a hacker will make it through all your defenses, and he's going to get to your endpoint. Especially with your users spread out across the United States, sitting at home, connecting to VPNs. So this is not an *if* question. It's a *when* question.

So when a hacker does bypass all the barriers you put up, what should you do?

One thing you shouldn't do is disable PowerShell, because most of your RMMs use it for automation. If you disable PowerShell, you'll be doing a lot more work than you are today, and you might not be able to keep up with your tickets. Another problem with disabling PowerShell is that all your server tools will be affected. Say you log in to Office 365, and you want to do something in Azure. You'll have to use PowerShell.

So what else can you do to prevent lateral movement?

You can focus on tokens and credentials. Put on your attacker hat for a moment. Pretend you hacked a computer and got in. You have access to the entire machine. You have a command line; you got all the shells; you're ready to go. The first thing you do is enumerate your environment—see what you've got access to. You look for things like accounts and passwords on the computer itself. Many of these will be in plain text or in the profile. You also look at cached accounts and browsers. You look at browser history to see if the user went anywhere interesting. And you look for credentials to figure out how much access the user has in the network.

The next thing you do, unless you're really lucky and phished your way into a domain administrator account on a server, is move. And the best way to move is to use the pass-the-hash technique.

Here's a quick recap on how it works. Most users are local admins on their own computers. Think about all the users you have out in the field who are local admins on their own computers. And a local admin can access the NTLM password hash. There's even a tool called Mimi Katz that does this for you. You type in a couple of commands, and *bam*— you have all these hashes. What do you do with them? You could crack them. You could run the hashes through a whole bunch of different letters and numbers for days on end. Sooner or later, you'll crack a hash and get in. But this is a pain in the rear.

Who has days to wait? You've got to move.

So you replay the password hash to a system service and convince it that you actually know the password. It's kind of crazy. Windows has this little flaw in its password implementation that lets you use a password on another machine if you know the hash, because these hashes are not salted. It's the same from computer to computer if the account password is the same. Let me be clear: this is only possible if there is an account password that's the same from computer to computer.

Most MSPs create a local admin account that's the same on every computer. This is why passing the hash is so successful on an MSP network. These user accounts are on each computer, and they usually share the username and password. That makes this type of attack super effective.

Why? Have you ever been working on your computer for a user, or you try to connect to a user's computer, and it's dropped off the domain? It's really hard to fix if you don't have a local admin account. So you pop onto it with the local admin account from your RMM tool, and then you can fix it.

So you're a hacker. You've got your local admin rights. Now what?

You can move through the network. You can find other machines. You can access stored things like credentials and hunt for cached browser passwords. You could do all this, but you don't have the holy grail. You only have local machine access. That means you won't be able to get to a whole lot of servers.

So you want to escalate privileges even further. You want to go for the domain admin account. That's how you can delete logs. That's how you move effortlessly through the environment. You can even access things like SQL Servers. But how do you get to domain admin when you only have local admin rights?

You start by finding a list of admins, a task for which you only need normal user credentials. A good way to do it is to abuse LDAP. You can get it to give you a list of all the users in groups. It will tell you when their passwords were last changed and all sorts of other stuff that will allow you to figure out where you might attack.

You then want to get onto a computer where there's a domain admin logged in. How do you do that? With a little thing called PowerView, which offers you a self-contained PowerShell environment where you can look around. It will give you a list of all the machines and who's logged in to them at that moment.

Then you use your local admin rights to move to a computer that has a domain admin logged in. You bring out that friendly little Mimi Katz program I mentioned above and use it to dump the hash of everybody who's logged in to the computer.

Now you have the hash for a domain admin, so you pass that hash to a shell. And that gets you domain admin rights.

With those domain admin rights, you own the world, or at least this network. You basically go wherever you want inside this network, hunting for data and backups. That's how a lot of attackers go through networks. They start out by getting local access, bypassing antivirus, escalating to domain admin, and then digging through a network.

What on earth should you do to keep this from happening?

- Don't use the same username and password on every computer.

- Log off your servers. Where do you think most domain admins are logged in when hackers look through a network? Servers. Why? Have you ever logged in to a server and found that somebody else has already logged in to it? And you had to boot somebody off in order to get access to it? That's because engineers have a really terrible habit of leaving themselves logged in. That puts the NTLM token right inside of memory for an attacker and identifies that machine as having had a domain admin logged in to it. It makes you a sitting duck for the pass-the-hash technique.

- Check your antivirus status and make sure it's running. Make sure it's getting updates. Make sure users can't disable it.

- Fix your local admin accounts. Come up with a script for your RMM that will eliminate password reuse.

- If you can, remove local admin rights for users.

I've got a quick mission for you; it should take around twenty minutes. Based on this chapter, create three alerts in RMM that you can use to protect your environment.

One of the easiest ways to determine whether your endpoint security is working as expected is to test it. And one of the easiest ways to test it is to check your alerts. For an effortless way to figure out what's working and what's not, and to help you come up with a plan, visit **GalacticScan.com/Stack**

CHAPTER 14
VIRUS REMOVAL

As you may know, there's a difference between a typical ransomware attack and an MSP-targeted attack. A normal ransomware attack is like a smash-and-grab—like when a burglar breaks into your car and grabs whatever he sees. Then he runs down the street.

MSP targeted attacks are more advanced, the attacker gets in and stays in. An advanced persistent threat, an APT, is more like a heist.

Do you remember *Ocean's Eleven*?

That was a crazy heist. Right? Eleven people were involved, each playing his or her own role and each offering his or her own skills. They all contributed and helped carry out the heist.

The plan involved trying to break into the Bellagio, the Mirage, and the MGM Grand all at once. And as you're watching the movie, you think they'll get caught. The final scenes? You're probably thinking, "Oh, my gosh, they're going to be captured." Remember? I don't want to spoil it for anyone, but the crew might have had a final trick up its sleeve.

That final trick, in an APT situation, is deploying ransomware.

If you're the victim, and you're sitting around restoring backups and trying to figure out whether to pay the ransom, there's one thing you're not doing, and that's going through forensics to see what data was stolen. You're not really looking to see what the heck happened. You just have way too much other work on your hands getting everything back online.

Anatomy of a Heist

Let's walk through how a heist actually works. The very first thing the organizer of an APT does is plan.

Put on your hacker hat for a moment and think back to *Ocean's Eleven*. First, you've got to have the right people on your team, because you need a bunch of different skills, not only to get in but also to enumerate the environment.

Then several other things have to happen. You have to build some infrastructure. You might need to stand up a new command and control network. You will need some sort of encryption mechanisms. There's a lot of building that goes on during the planning phase. You also need to acquire the necessary tools. Maybe that means developing custom code, maybe creating custom PowerShell scripts, maybe buying some zero-day vulnerabilities.

The next step is getting into the network. The easiest way to do this has usually been through social engineering—tricking a user into clicking on a link. That's been the number one way for a long, long time, but recently there's been a huge uptick in attackers using credentials to get into networks. They obtain passwords used for VPN access, because there's a whole bunch of patches out there for various firewalls. (see the chapter on firewalls)

Just like software, all firewall vendors have vulnerabilities in their products. Let me give you a quick example of one that can be compromised with an HTTP request. Basically, the hacker sends a special HTTP request to a device. It dumps all the passwords of every user who has ever logged in through VPN on that device. Those passwords are showing up on the dark web right now. Because, well, these passwords are really easy to harvest. Even the most novice programmer can create a little crawler that walks all the IPv4 addresses and tries to connect to a specific URL. (Hint: make sure you're getting your firewall firmware updated, and update those passwords.) Even more scary, many of these passwords are not even making it to the dark web, so you don't have a chance of knowing if you are compromised

As the hacker, the next thing you do once you get into the network is persist. In other words, you can't just get in, you have to get in and stay in. How do you access a network? Pass yourself a command line, called a shell, where you can tell the computer that you are accessing to run programs. This works much like your RMM. Next, you'll want to have a tool that will open the shell back up if you get disconnected. It could be on a timer. Every couple of hours it could open up a connection for you to remotely control the computer. It doesn't have to be on all the time, just every few hours. You are going to want to use a shell that isn't used by all the other hackers out there, because all the antiviruses will recognize it. This is where that custom code comes in.

Hackers have investors, just like the *Ocean's Eleven* crew did. And when I say investors, I'm talking nation-states, cartels and even other hackers. They have the vast resources necessary to build their own tools, or to create purpose designed tools for single missions.

Okay, so you are in the network, and you've established persistence. The next thing you want to do is find the gold mines of data on the network—that is, unless you're really lucky and your phishing expedition landed you on an IT person's device or maybe the CFO's computer. If that doesn't happen, and it never seems to work out that way, you have to expand and move laterally across the network.

The next thing you do as a hacker is evade. As a hacker you don't to lose the huge investment you've already made into this heist. This means creating smokescreens so people can't see you moving through the network. There are a couple of ways to do this. One is to obfuscate where your attack is coming from by running your traffic through a connection the network makes often. You could do this by connecting back to servers in Azure for example. Think about that for a minute. If you, the hacker, routed all your traffic through Azure, what else goes to the Azure servers? Microsoft 365 traffic, One Drive traffic, remote control session to Azure infrastructure, maybe even Azure AD calls. This is a lot of traffic that you can hide in.

Now pretend you're the good guy. Let's say you're responsible for identifying and stopping any crazy network traffic that might try to get through. You probably want to automatically block all the hacker's bad IP addresses.

But with Azure, that's a different story. If you block Azure, guess what happens? You get some pretty upset users who can't get to their OneDrive or their e-mail. So not only do you have to let that traffic through, but if you're doing deep packet inspection, can you even keep up? Most environments that run deep packet inspection have exclusions for Azure because they don't have the throughput to handle services like OneDrive. Inspecting all the Azure bound traffic would be a pretty heavy load on the firewall. So the attacker can assume that there's lower chance of being seen if he's moving to and from Azure. This isn't just an Azure problem. If any of your clients have AWS environments, or they're using AWS servers, you're in a similar situation. It's very easy for a hacker to avoid detection if you're routing traffic through Azure, AWS, and even Google.

Now your hacker hat is back on. You've got your team deployed. They're in all the various places they need to be. You've got to get to the goodies, right?

You're looking for personal data, intellectual property, classified intel, confidential communications. If you're an APT going after an MSP, you're looking for access to their clients, too. You're looking for runbooks and any type of data you can use. You're looking for best access to the RMMs. During this phase you're looking for data that you can access and exfiltrate or tools you can use for the next phase.

At this point, you may move to the next phase by one of two triggers. The first one is an alarm going off. The second is finding something of value. Something of high value. Maybe it is a patient list at a medical practice. Maybe it is client access at an MSP. When you find it, and you get it out of the environment, it's time to get out. How do you get out? You're going to drop a bomb to cover your tracks. This will make it nearly impossible for the victim to understand what you've done, taken, or accessed. It's time to detonate that ransomware payload.

So what are the signs that something fishy is going on? Let's move back to protecting your networks and clients.

The first is late-night logins. I was just on a call with a security vendor who said he sees the largest number of attacks in the SOC late at night, typically between 6:00 p.m. on Fridays and 3:00 a.m. on Sundays. Attackers know that's when the skeleton crew comes on.

But in fact, this vendor said, he puts his best and brightest on the weekend shifts because that's when attacks are most likely to happen. If you're running a SOC, you might want to consider this as well.

You also might want to educate your team—give them a heads-up and ask them to watch for this stuff (most techs are not focused on identifying suspicious activity).

You should be alerting for late-night logins—especially if you start to see many of them or if those late-night logins stay on for extended periods of time.

You also might see an increase in spear phishing, originating either internally, or, in some cases, externally. That's another pretty good indicator that you have something going on. But we've seen an uptick in phishing overall, so be careful when making the determination that you have an attacker on your network.

You might also start seeing malware frequently picked up on a particular network. That might mean that hackers are experimenting with various tools and tactics. This is a good indicator that you have a ghost in the machine—that it's more than just a drive-by smash-and-grab and that you actually have a heist going on. If you see three malware events in a week, take a closer look. Keep in mind, it might not always pop up on the same user or machine. I would suggest creating an alert that counts the number of times malware happens in each of the environments you support over a rolling 10-day period.

In addition, you might look for data flows to new places, which indicate a compromised network. Let's say, for example, that all of a sudden you start seeing a bunch of data go into Microsoft 365. It is time to trace that back and look at which machines show suspicious data flows.

Finally, look for an increase in computer usage. An increase in processor time indicates that somebody may be attempting to crack passwords or cyphers. You should be able to do this with your monitoring tools.

Removing Malware
How do you remove malware safely?

The answer depends on what type of client has the malware—basic, security-conscious, or compliance-driven (see page 85).

But first, I'm going to assume that you have the following three best practices in place.

- **The first imperative is to back up your data**. If you don't, you're not prepared to recover from a ransomware event—or any type of event, for that matter.

  You should have several tools in place to back up your data. It's like having two parachutes: if the first one doesn't deploy, you always have the second.

  Let me be clear: backups do not protect data from hackers. They simply allow you to recover from a successful ransomware detonation.

- **The second imperative is to employ image backup** or an image-build process—some way to quickly rebuild every computer in your environment.

- Finally, **you need to have local admin accounts to be able to access the computer with administrative rights**. Remember: you should use a different password for each computer in the field.

Now that you have those three things in place, it's time to work through a process for removing malware.

First, if you're performing this task for a client who's compliance-driven, my suggestion is simple: **follow the organization's breach response or incident-response protocol**. Do not trust your gut, do not clean it up and move on. Just follow their protocol.

That protocol very likely has a section on taking a forensic image of the data. The easiest and fastest way to do this is to pull the drives and replace them with new ones. In other words, take the drive out of the computer, put it into an evidence bag, label it, and put a new drive in place. Then image the computer, and restore the data. Make sure to keep a log or a journal as you are doing this. Your normal ticket process will work great. Document events like, the time you removed a particular drive, who did the work.

After you are done restoring the backup, flush the temporary files. Do a virus scan, and ask the users to change all their passwords. And change your local admin password on each device.

Obviously, do not mount the drive containing the original evidence you took out and dropped in the evidence bag. If you start it up on an operating system, even if you just mount it, you run a risk of damaging it. Really important! Just drop it in the bag, seal it, then maintain it for the amount of time that the client's incident-response policy mandates.

For security-conscious clients, my suggestion is to **engage them in a discussion before an incident occurs** about whether to create forensic images of their devices—maybe at your next quarterly business review, or maybe just the next time you talk with them. Ask them if they want evidence of malware and the ability to track it down later. If they say yes, then follow the procedure above.

If they say no, then skip the drive removal and reimage the computers. I would not actually spend any time removing malware. Just reimage the drive, restore the data you have backed up, perform a scan on the computers, and force the users to change their passwords. Next change the local admin password for that client's computers. Since all of them have different passwords, and you are pushing the password out with a script from your RMM per earlier recommendations, this should be very easy for you.

What about the basic-needs clients? You may want to remove the malware rather than reimage the computer. In these situations, I see folks doing a few things wrong during virus removals. First, they log in to a computer with domain admin credentials just to take a look around and see what's going on. If an attacker doesn't have admin rights yet, that tech has just given him what he needs to get that domain admin password. The hacker doesn't even have to be keylogging to get the domain admin rights.

Have you ever tried to log in to a computer that was joined to a domain but not connected to the network? You probably noticed that it lets you log in even if it cannot reach the domain, as long as you have logged into the computer before with this account while the computer was connected to the network. This is pretty darn handy, because otherwise laptops wouldn't work very well. If you took them off-site, you wouldn't be able to log in.

Here's what's going on. The computer caches everyone who logs in to it on the domain in something called the Security Account Manager (SAM). This is a database that is present on computers running the Windows operating system. If you gain access to this database and dump the hashes out of it, you can get the hash for any user that ever logged into the computer.

Why is that a big deal? Because an attacker can use the hash for two things. He can take it back with him and put it in the lab and beat on it until he finds a password that works and matches it. Or he can pass that hash directly to a network pipe and move onto any device that allows that account to log in to it, because Microsoft thinks he already knows that password, that he's already entered it in.

This is really important. ***Never* log in to a user's computer with a domain administrative credentials.** Let me clarify: if a user logs in to the computer, do not use domain admin credentials to log in to it. Instead, use local admin credentials. You can do everything you need to do on a machine with local admin credentials. If it is a server, and users do not log into it with either a console session or a remote desktop session, you can use your domain administrative credentials to log into it. Also, when you are logged in as a local administrator and you need to access network resources, you can use your domain administrative rights to access these. The login event is when your credentials get cached in the local SAM database.

Let's get to removing the malware. How do you do that? (By the way, you should have a procedure in your organization for removing malware. If you don't, you should draw one up right about now.)

First, check to make sure you have a backup. If you don't have a backup, stop what you're doing, pull the drive, and put a new drive in. That way you can pull in the data you need off that original drive, and it's much easier than trying to make a backup with a device or with a computer that's already having problems.

Next, enable safe mode with networking. To do that, boot the machine inside with the boot options RP. Choose "startup settings," and then select safe mode with networking.

The next step is to actually remove the malware.

When it gets around to coming up, it will ask you for a login prompt, and you should use a local admin login. Remember, this is the local admin account I mentioned above, the one that has different credentials for every computer in the network. If it doesn't, you will potentially give access to an attacker. So just be very, very careful that there are different passwords on every single machine.

Next, run an antivirus scan.

After that, check startup items. This could include the registry, the scheduler, and the startup items folder. There are a whole bunch of places you can look to make sure startup is covered. List all those places in your procedure.

Next, add back the damaged files. There are probably a number of Windows files that were damaged. You can do this by opening a command line. I suggest bringing up CMD.exe, right-click on it, and run it as an administrator, because you need to have admin credentials to perform the next steps.

Now at the command prompt type in: sfc /scannow

Those are the steps you'll take on the computer, but you're not done yet.

Next, update the local admin password in case it was likely accessed by whoever was on the machine. Update it on the computer itself, and update it in your password manager so the next person can get in.

Finally, ask users to reset all their passwords. When I say this, people assume I am only talking about the passwords to access the computer. I suggest you have the user update the password they use for personal websites, vendor sites, cloud services, social media, bank accounts, and anything else they have ever accessed from this machine.

The most important thing is to follow your procedure, which should match the type of client you're working with.

Here's a quick mission for you:

Review and update your incident-response procedure.
If you don't have such a procedure, now is the time to create one.

For a quick primer on creating a solid incident-response plan, visit **GalacticScan.com/Incident-Response**.

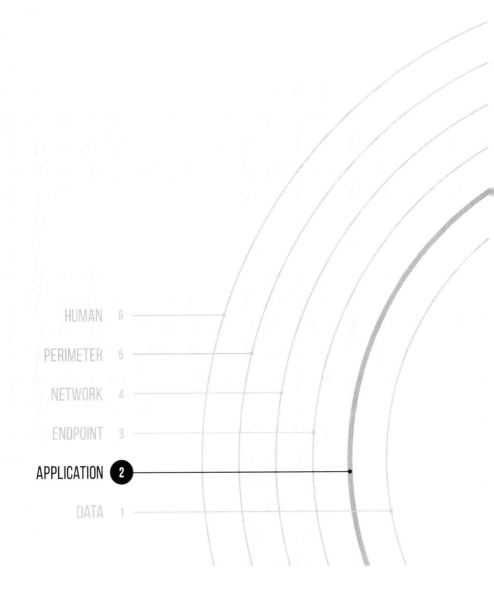

HUMAN 6

PERIMETER 5

NETWORK 4

ENDPOINT 3

APPLICATION 2

DATA 1

APPLICATIONS

One of the biggest challenges I faced when I was scaling my MSP was creating a way to easily maintain our clients' applications. That means having a well-oiled patch process and securely using your RMM to do the work.

CHAPTER 15
PATCH PROCEDURES

Patching sucks.

We all hate it. It's a thankless job. It's never finished. It's the bane of every IT person's existence. We all have to deal with it, though. So let's talk about why we have to patch.

Programmers make mistakes—I lead a team of them, and I speak from firsthand experience.

When a programmer messes up, it isn't necessarily a big deal unless he leaves something open. Now we have a vulnerability. Then either a hacker finds it or somebody on the security side finds it and reports it. Now we have a vulnerability and possibly an exploit for that vulnerability. What happens next? Someone has to create a patch for the vulnerability. Then all the people running the software have to get the patch and install it. Simple, right?

Imagine if you found a vulnerability in the lock on your front door. If you jiggled it back and forth and you pushed down on it real hard, the door would open up. That would be a pretty big vulnerability.

So you report the flaw to the manufacturer of the lock, who says, "Thanks. Here's a new half-inch shaft that you can install to fix it." But then the manufacturer goes around your neighborhood and posts pictures of that lock with an announcement that says if you jiggle the handle back and forth and push on it real hard, it'll open up.

Every crook and bad guy in your neighborhood is going to know exactly how to get into those particular locks. They'd be able to hunt down the lock on your front door and open it up.

Why would the manufacturer do that? Because they want to let the owners of the locks know that they need to buy that little shaft. That replacement shaft is our patch.

Put on your hacker hat for a minute. Let's say you just worked your magic. You got somebody to click on a link and you socially engineered your way in. But the IT department or the MSP that's supporting this environment did the right thing. None of the local users had admin rights over their computers. So you land on the machine, and you only have user access rights. As an attacker this isn't any fun. You are stuck. You're stuck in userland with no access or ability to move laterally.

We all know that you can't do much in userland. The only thing you can do is search the data you have access to. Maybe you get some Social Security numbers, credit card numbers, whatever that user has. But to really move throughout the environment, you're going to have to escalate your privileges.

The first thing you do is bring up the command prompt. After you do that, you see a cursor blinking at you and you type in "system info." Most of you guys know that command already. Now a bunch of data is pouring across the screen too quickly for you to see it all.

About halfway through, you're going to see the HotFixes installed. This tells you all the patches that have been installed on the machine.

How do you go from a HotFix to a vulnerability? If you've ever looked this up, you'll know it's a real pain in the rear to figure out what vulnerabilities are covered by what HotFix, because there a number of different combinations you could use to get the coverage.

What do you do as a hacker? You download a nifty little tool. My favorite is one called Windows Exploit Suggester—a simple Python script. You run it, and you type in "system info" and export the data to a file called "systeminfo.txt." Next you get that "systeminfo.txt" and you run the Windows Exploit Suggester. Voilà! You have the list of exploits for this computer. This script looks at a database you can download from Microsoft. It compares it against bulletins and tells you what to exploit.

You might notice vulnerabilities in Windows kernel mode, or drivers that could allow elevation of privilege. These vulnerabilities are not marked as a critical patch.

You look through the vulnerability list, find one that gives you some escalation of privileges, and you're off to the races. You get yourself some local admin privileges, and you take those local admin privileges and pass the hash (see page 137).

That's why you, as the MSP, want to patch. We're not just talking about patching computers and servers. We're not just talking about patching operating systems. We're also talking about patching software.

As the hacker, what if, instead of doing all the work I just did, you were able to open a PDF and get admin rights that way?

Quick question: Did you install Acrobat using administrative rights? If you did it through an RMM, chances are very high that you did. Have you ever considered how many things in your environment need patching to keep them from being attacked?

Let's look at the numbers: 21,000 new vulnerabilities between January 2019 and June 2020. That's over 1,100 new vulnerabilities per month. We're talking about vulnerabilities in operating systems, firmware, and enterprise systems. We're not talking about your iPhone and other personal devices. We're only talking about things used in businesses.

In 2019, 57 percent of cyberattack victims admitted that applying a specific patch would have prevented an attack altogether. Fifty-seven percent! That's more than half! Think about that. Think about how many patches are out there that you haven't applied. Or how many machines are out there that are missing patches.

That brings up another number—102. That's the average number of days it takes to patch something. We have ourselves an issue here, and we have a lot of work to do.

Rather than throwing Microsoft under the bus, which is always really easy when it comes to patching, let me talk a bit about Adobe. Why am I picking on Adobe? Because I want you to think like a hacker.

How will you achieve the highest return on your investment? By going after Adobe Acrobat? Or by going after some sort of vertical-specific software that may only be installed on a few computers? Think about it from a numbers standpoint. Would you want to write a tool to attack a piece of software that's in 5 percent of your targets? Or something that's installed in more like 90 percent of your targets? This is why we're choosing to talk about Acrobat: because a lot of people out there use it.

An advisory was issued late in 2019. It stated that vulnerabilities in Adobe Acrobat could result in arbitrary code execution. It went a little further and said these vulnerabilities could allow a user to create, manipulate, print, and maybe manage files. It indicated that a successful exploitation could result in an attacker gaining control of the affected system. Depending on the privileges associated with user, the attack could be severe.

Why am I bringing this up? Because patches, as they're released from the manufacturer, use weak, passive language. You have to read four paragraphs to get any indication that you are at risk. They don't say what they really should say: "Look out! An attacker will use this to get administrative rights on your computer and pown your a$$."

In my opinion. If they did—if the people discovering the patches and notifying us about them shared our sense of urgency—the average patch cycle would probably shrink from 102 days down to ten.

. . . .

Which are the most important patches when it comes to updating the computers you support? The ones an attacker uses to get into your system, right?

Focus your effort on the most popular programs. If you miss a patch on a piece of software everyone uses like Microsoft Windows versus the software that only your organization uses like an industry specific practice management software you will be at higher risk of being exploited.

A word of caution before we continue.

When we're analyzing networks, we often see MSPs with issues applying Feature Updates. We might see older build numbers like 17763, we're a little cautious. We tell the MSP, "This is an issue, because those versions no longer get support." That means that even though you are applying patches to this particular Feature Update, it's not getting them. Most RMMs out there will show that the machine is completely patched and up to date, because there are no more patches for this operating system. Bottom line – be careful when it comes to unsupported operating systems. Your tools will tell you that they are "up to date" because they have all the patches available to them applied...but no new patches are being released.

If you think your machines are patched and they're really not, that generates all sorts of problems for your operations. So draw up a list of any machines that are running older builds and start upgrading them.

Inventory the software systems in your environment. Use this list to create a report that shows all the software that's installed. You should be able to see how many copies of each are out there. Once you have that, do the same for the hardware. Next, set up an email address. You can call it something like "Patching@YourDomain.com." This is where patch notifications can go. Sign up with all the vendors that show up on the list you created.

Google each of your vendors to find out where to sign up for security notifications. For example, you can get the information from Microsoft's technical security notifications and Adobe's security notifications. They will be happy to send you an email when they have a critical patch. Do this for your RMM and other tools like your document management system.

After you do that, it's time to put together your patching process.

I'm going to focus on the steps you need to take regardless of vendor. It doesn't matter what RMM you use—you need to go through all these same steps. If you have somebody doing this for you, that person should go through the same steps, too.

First, test the patches on yourself.

A lot of people will tell you to stand up a lab and put the test patch in the lab, make sure it works, then send the patches out to your team to see whether anything blows up. If you create a patch test lab, you will have a difficult time figuring out if something is actually broken.

My recommendation is to test the patches on the users in your organization. I recommend you patch your computers on Tuesday nights. Late at night. Roll out the test patches out in your environment first.

On Wednesday morning, when people on your team are coming in, check with them. How are things working?

Then, the following Wednesday night, **test the patches on a small group of users in your client base**. Communicate with them about it first. I would suggest having one or two primary contacts, maybe technical contacts, at each of your client locations. Explain it to them and say, "Hey, we want to make sure these patches are working properly, so we're going to roll them out to you first, on Wednesday nights. Then we'll roll them out to the rest of your team on Thursdays."

Why are you doing this? Because the fact that you tested the patches in your own environment doesn't mean they'll work in your clients' environments. You're not running all the same tools and all the same software as your clients are.

Finally, on Thursday night, **deploy all the patches out in the field**. (Deploy them to users and workstations, not to servers.)

Then **validate the patches** to confirm that they're in place. This is an important step that's often skipped. Create a report inside your RMM that you can use to confirm patch deployment. Next, patch your servers. We recommend doing this on Sunday Nights. Make sure to communicate to your users and set up an outage window. Apply the patches, then validate they were installed and test to make sure you can access the server when you are done. You may also want to verify the services you expect are back online.

Alerting

I was inspired to write this section after an MSP reached out to me in the wake of an incident involving one of its clients.

The client was hacked and had to pay a significant ransom.

A forensics team investigated, and a question came up: Would event-based alerting have helped this situation? And the answer is absolutely. The attackers were in the environment for over 4 weeks before they detonated ransomware.

Just a couple of reminders here. First, having the default settings for Windows Auditing is a bare minimum. Very few alerts will come out of your standard default Active Directory settings. Why? Event logs take up space.

You should set up the maximum-security log size. If you have a pretty big environment, as most of our clients do, you probably want to set this to around four gigs. You should also set your system log size to four gigs. You might be thinking, "Wow—that'll slow things down. I'm going to have these huge logs that take a really long time to open."

I'm not the log police. I'm just a guy who's just giving you some recommendations! But take it from me: my recommendations are based on experience. Opening a four-gig log may take a long time, but you are going to want that data if you ever experience an event.

After you've set up those logs, and after you set up the audit alerts, and after you set up the account lockout, you'll realize that you have yourself a whole lot of noise. You'll get a lot of event-log entries. That's why you set your log size to four gigs.

Attackers know that people are looking for them, so they don't exactly say, "Here I am!" They hide in very, very specific entries, so you'll be looking for very specific event IDs.

I want to lay out the assumptions I'm making in this chapter. The first is that you use current event IDs rather than the legacy event IDs that are out there. If you're running Windows 2003, and you've got a Windows 2003 server on your network, too bad! You'll have to google the solution yourself or figure it out somehow. Maybe it's just time to upgrade the darn thing.

I also assume you have a RMM—a tool that allows remote monitoring and management of all the computers you support. Now, this can be all sorts of different things. It doesn't matter what you use, as long as it has the ability to filter through event logs and create alerts or tickets based on certain event IDs.

Another assumption is that your Windows events flow into your RMM and that you're saving them in your event logs and archiving them.

Keep in mind that even though I'm only talking about Windows in this chapter, it's not the only thing you should be monitoring for compromises in your environment. You should also be monitoring firewalls and other elements of your cyber stack. Setting up Windows alerts is one piece of your strategy for finding active threats inside your environment, but it is by no means the only piece.

I have a few objectives:

- I want to you to be able to **pick up clues** that an attacker is in your environment. If there's a ghost in the machine, what kind of evidence does he leave? What types of events occur?

- I want you to **start simply**. Do not turn on all of your alerts at once.

- I want you to **test the alerting techniques in your own environment** before you roll them out to your clients so you can determine whether they'll have an impact on your performance.

- I want you to **recognize what false alarms look like**.

Do you remember Where's Waldo?

Good luck trying to find him. He's only one person in a huge group of people engaged in all kinds of activities. But that's what alerting is about: instead of looking through all kinds of data trying to find Waldo, you're going to describe Waldo to your event system so it can pick out the events that look most like him—the clues that will help you find an attacker in your system.

Keep in mind, though, that there's a big difference between the game and real life. In the game, you assume that Waldo is on every page. In real life, Waldo might not be there at all. You might have some false positives. That's okay, as long as you don't spend all day looking through false positives.

I've said several times in this book that you should test your processes and tools in your own environments before you test them in your clients' environments, and alerting is no exception. It's like what flight attendants tell you on an airplane: put on your own oxygen mask before you help someone else. That's because if you pass out, you won't be any use to the person next to you.

But an airline flight is not really the right metaphor for this chapter, because in this case you're more like the pilot than the passengers: you have to have a better oxygen mask than the people you're supporting do.

Think about a commercial airline pilot. He doesn't have one of these little garbage oxygen masks the passengers have. He has a really good one. It has dual airflow and a whole bunch of other things to prevent him from losing consciousness. Because if he loses consciousness and the plane falls out of the sky, all the people who are wearing the garbage masks will fall right along with him.

So improve the security posture inside your MSP first. And make your oxygen mask better than the ones your clients wear. Remember that you are the weakest link. You are the one who has access to all the individual workstations and devices you support. Start your event log monitoring on your MSP and then slowly expand it to your clients.

Now that you've set up your event logs and alerts, let's look at specific event IDs. (Remember, these are recent, current event IDs.) I'm assuming that as these IDs come in, they're being aggregated back to your [fill in the blank] or to some sort of system where you can keep all your event IDs in one spot. Why? Because we're looking for clues to an attacker in your environment.

Event ID 4740

Let's start with event ID 4740. This is the one that says, "Hey, there have been too many log-in attempts for one particular account, and it's been locked out."

This is a good one: it means that you don't have to worry about somebody cracking into your system. Another reason this is important is that if you start seeing a whole bunch of missed password attempts, somebody might have opened an RDP session to the outside world. Or maybe one of the machines in your environment has some malware on it that's trying to log in or attack.

In this case, maybe reach out to the user and help him or her log on. Because if you're the user who just got locked out, wouldn't it be cool if you got a phone call from somebody saying, "We noticed that you got locked out of the system. Just want to make sure you're okay. Are you trying to log on right now? What's going on?"

That will help you with threat detection *and* will improve client experience, so 4740 is a good one to monitor.

Basically, your RMM will pick up those log-in attempts from the workstation and move them up to a database. Inside the database, you have a rule that's looking for 4740. When it finds it, it creates a ticket, prompting you to investigate.

Event ID 4649

The next thing you'll want to look at is event ID 4649. It's a sequence that's used to log in to another device. This is usually triggered by bad software—a problem with the software itself. It's not usually triggered by an attacker, but it's a good idea to keep an eye out for it anyway. If you're seeing these 4649 events, figure out what's creating it and get rid of it. Exit and update the software.

A lot of times this is generated when Microsoft updates the operating system. Maybe you're missing an update for one of your tools, which is then creating this 4649 event. Obviously, this is not always an indicator of compromise.

Event ID 4719

The next thing you'll want to watch for is event ID 4719. This comes up when the system audit policy gets changed.

Now, why would that matter? Because if an attacker gets in, he may want to modify the system audit policy.

If an attacker doesn't want to get caught, he can do one of two things: he can either do the things he's going to do and then try to cover his tracks, or if he sees that the person who's running the network has tools in place that are aggregating in a log somewhere that he's not able to destroy, he can modify the system's audit policy so that he doesn't get picked up, or his behavior doesn't get picked up. So this is definitely something you want to keep an eye out for.

Obviously, you need to be careful. Don't start looking for this event while you're setting up your audits. If you set up your audit policy, it's going to trigger this event.

Also, a good way to test your alerting is to set this event up and then trigger it to make sure it goes all the way up the system and creates a ticket for your team to look into.

However, you want to be very careful to not blow up your team with tickets. So if you create a separate board, you can put these events on it for a while before you start incorporating them into your help-desk flow.

Event IDs 4765 and 4766

If you're not actively migrating accounts between domains, setting up new domains and migrating them, or merging a few domains, then event IDs 4765 and 4766 signal that an attacker potentially has the option to abuse his privileges. I would suggest setting up this event and monitoring for it.

Event ID 4765 means a domain has been added. Event ID 4766 means that the migration has failed. Either way, you'll want to look at what's going on.

Event ID 4794

The next event ID is 4794, triggered when somebody puts your server in Active Directory Services Restore Mode. This means either that there's something naughty going on or something's broken and somebody's going to fix it. Either way, you should create an alert for this, because it won't be super noisy.

One of the things attackers try to always get their hands on are these directory services. If they start to put them in restore mode, this is a good indicator that they're up to no good.

Event ID 4964

If all of a sudden a new member gets added to a special group such as domain admins, you'll want to know what's going on. You will also want to look for Event ID 4727, 4735, and 4737.

Event IDs 4771 and 4625

You should also check to see whether you've got some log-in fails, which you can do with event IDs 4771 and 4625. And you absolutely have to filter for hex 18, which signals a bad password.

Why is this important? You could have a user who's entering her password wrong over and over. It could be an Exchange Server hosted locally. Maybe somebody's iPad has the wrong password on it. But it could also be a pass-the-hash attack in progress or a hacker attempting to brute-force a login.

Event ID 4648

The next event ID you might want to look for is 4648. This usually shows up when somebody's trying to use explicit credentials that are different from the ones originally assigned.

You've done that before: you right clicked on an application, then ran as, or you've tried to run something as somebody else on the domain.

How often do your users do that, though? How often do your users use explicit credentials? Probably not that often, right? The only reason they would do that is if you set up a shortcut for them. And no, I can't remember ever doing that in our organization. I think this is a pretty safe event ID to look for.

Let's say you're a hacker who used the pass-the-hash technique to land on a machine, but it's only for a local user and you want additional credentials. You'd try various credentials to see which one gives you the rights you want. Definitely something to look for while you're hunting.

Event ID 4672

You also want to look for instances at which special privileges are assigned to a new login. This means somebody added someone to the domain admin groups.

Your mission is to create an alert for a special group assignment. This is event ID 4964 inside your RMM so that you can see it, you've got in the situation where there's been a special group assignment inside your infrastructure. Then assign administrative privileges to one of your users. Does the alert fire?

If you're struggling with a patch procedure or want to compare yours with one that hundreds of MSPs have tested and contributed to, visit **GalacticScan.com/Patch-Procedure**.

CHAPTER 16
RMM HARDENING

Your RMM is the most critical piece
of your overall infrastructure.

This is the tool you use to access the computers you support. This is
the tool you use to remote control computers. You use it to run scripts
on your clients. It can also do things like enforce group policy, reset
passwords, and patch computers. All sorts of things are possible with
this tool. And because of that, it has to have very high-end privileges
on all of the computers, networks and servers you support.

When you think of your RMM, you probably think of just one tool
you use to do this type of work, but there are more. Think about all
the tools out there that have this level of access—tools that run with
system account, or higher privileges, things that are way beyond a
normal user's capability. All of the different tools that have the ability
to execute commands or remotely access your client computers.

Did you know that most antivirus can push a script to the computer and
execute it? Even backup solutions can push scripts to computers and
execute them. There are all sorts of tools that can be used against you.
And if a hacker gets in to any one of these, he can really mess up your day.

Can you imagine being stuck on a rooftop and not being able to get
down? That would suck, right? Now imagine an attacker using your
remote-access tools to lock you out of your own workstation.
The same kind of situation, right?

Think like a hacker for a minute. How would you get in? You probably
wouldn't spend a lot of time brute forcing it. You'd probably just aim for
the phish. Right? If you haven't noticed, that's the easiest way to get in.
We see it all the time. In fact, 90 percent of attacks start with the phish,
and 11 percent of helpdesk engineers are phished each year. Phish
your way in, establish persistence, find out what you've got, then attack.

As a hacker, what if you went phishing and found that you have access
to ninety businesses instead of just one? Imagine the payoff you would

see from being able to ransom ninety businesses at once. Basically, you could retire. Just think: ninety businesses would pay $175,000 each. Or maybe you could ransom the MSP itself for $1.5 million. These are the numbers we're seeing when it comes to this type of event.

. . . .

I'm going to introduce you to your mission now rather than wait until the end of the chapter. Your mission is to create a checklist—a list of things to look at on your RMM as you review your infrastructure.

But first, take out that original list you made in chapter 16. Do something similar here: jot down all the tools in your environment by name. What do you use for antivirus? Write it down. What are you using for backups? What are you using for remote control? What do you use for remote access? Make a list of each tool you're currently using.

At the top of the list will be your RMM tool. Now beside each of these tools, indicate if they have the ability to run scripts on computers in your environment. The ones that do are the ones you will be focusing on for this mission.

You're probably thinking, "I'm an engineer, and I should have access to everything at all times." But think about your domain login. You don't log in to your computer with your domain admin credentials. You don't use the credentials that can do things like create new users and reset other people's passwords with your daily access account. Instead, you use a lower privileged account. A day-to-day user account. I want you to think about your RMM in the same way.

You're going to set up four different permission levels. These are very simple. Some of you might protest: "But Bruce, I'm a one-man-show. I'm a one-man-MSP. I'm a one-man-IT department. I don't need to do this; trust me."

Two things, first a hacker doesn't care if you are a one person IT department or a 40 person IT department. They want access to your clients. Second, you probably won't be a one-man band for long. You definitely want to take the time to do this. Especially before you start hiring more people for your team.

Okay, back to the permission levels. The first level is for your administrative users. They have access to everything in the environment. They can alter security settings. They can remote into your own IT assets. As in they can remote into the computers at your office. They're able to do things like change passwords, and they have all sorts of privileged responsibility inside the RMM itself.

You should only have two or three accounts like this, and those people should use their normal accounts, their normal user-level accounts, for their day-to-day work and use this administrative account only when they're making changes within the RMM itself. For example if they are adding a new user or possibly approving scripts for others on your team to use.

The next permission level you will want is for the people who will be developing scripts on your team. You're going to have automation: scripts that make it so your team doesn't have to do everything themselves. These are the folks who have the ability to create scripts, run scripts, and assign permissions to scripts.

You may want to lock these users down so they can only run scripts in test computers. Now, your mileage will vary with that, so you can decide whether that's how you want to do it. Of course, I recommend that you create a test environment for your developers.

The third level is for your support users—the people who are able to run scripts already published by your developers. They're able to access all machines except those in the IT support environment —i.e., the machines that are your own assets. They can connect to client computers and support external users, but they're not going to be able to log in to another technician's computer, for example.

Finally, there is the internal support level. If you have an IT director you support, or maybe one of your clients has a few internal IT support members. These would be set up with the internal support permission level inside your RMM.

Whereas support users will be able to access all the computers in the environment, internal support users will only be able to access computers within their own companies. You might not want to give them the ability to run scripts, because once you do, you open a can of worms from a security standpoint.

Okay, now that you have the security levels set up, you have a little more work to do. If you use custom fields to store data, you will want to set up permissions on them. You also want to set up proper permissions for your custom scripts. For example, if you have a script that creates a new administrator on a domain, you may not want everybody to be able to run that.

Next, for all of these tools, not just your RMM you will want to make sure you have multifactor authentication configured. Here's an example of why this is important: while I was writing this book, I was auditing an antivirus console for an MSP. They had everything configured properly, just the way I wanted to see it. However, the multifactor authentication wasn't set up right. Initially, they turned on for all users. But one of the users had an issue—her iPhone was damaged. I don't know exactly how, but she said it was broken. So her manager turned off the multifactor authentication on her account so she could work.

After the multifactor authentication was disabled she went back to work. A few days later, she got a new phone. And on the new device, the multifactor authentication never got turned back on. Even though It was properly set up, and everybody had it, it was disabled for one user. My point is that it's very easy for somebody to have a reason to disable multifactor authentication. Another way this ends up getting disabled is when a new user is created and it never gets set up in the first place.

You are going to want to go in and verify multifactor authentication is set up on no less than a quarterly basis. While you're looking at multifactor authentication, there are a bunch of other things you can and should modify. The first is your roster of users. Make sure it contains the users who should have access to the system. If there's somebody on that list who hasn't been an employee for two years, you've got a problem. If there's somebody you don't recognize, figure out why that person is there or disable the account until you can investigate.

The next thing you should have is a password policy. I know everybody says you don't need a password policy if you have multifactor authentication. But I don't buy that, and here's why: when you have multifactor authentication and somebody does something silly like cache a password on a web browser, an attacker can get that password. Now that the attacker has the password, all they need is the multifactor token. Think about some of the services that allow you to authenticate from a web browser. Does any of your team use those services? There are lots of ways for an attacker to get around to an authenticator token. Be very careful to rotate your passwords on no less than a 90-day cycle even if you have multifactor authentication in place.

In addition, you need a lockout period. An idle period of time before the tool locks the user out. We don't want anybody to leave an RMM open on an unattended computer for an extended amount of time. At minimum, set the lockout period for sixty minutes. This is different than the computer lock idle timeout period. We are looking for something specifically in the RMM tool to lock the user out.

Next, set the failed login attempts to five or fewer. Even though we are talking about IT people, these users still set passwords like "Username2021!," . If an attacker sees a password on the dark web like "Username2020!," he might try changing the year to 2021. This is why you want to have some sort of failed login attempts set. If someone is attempting passwords they find on the dark web we want them to run out of tries quickly.

A note of caution: on one occasion, we were auditing an MSP, and the lead engineer set his password to "Welcome1!" You're probably wondering why that would ever happen.

When the MSP hired him, the company set his password to "Welcome1!," and he never got around to changing it. He was afraid something would break inside the system if he changed it, He was concerned that he might lock himself out, so he just left it. Snafus like this happen all the time, your goal is to protect your business from them. Every account you set up, you should create a random string. This goes for client users as well as your own employees. You should be setting random strings, not things like "Welcome1!." You want passwords that are hard to type and hard to remember. If users never get around to changing them, at least they'll have really strong passwords.

The next thing I want you to do is set up auditing.

At the very least, you want to have something that creates a list of failed log-in attempts and user log-in events. When people log in, you want to see not only that they logged in but also where they logged in from and other details. I suggest you create an audit event for script execution and remote-control access, too, so whenever somebody accesses a machine remotely, there's a record of it.

Finally, if you're storing passwords in your RMM, you should have some sort of audit to record whenever anybody looks up or uses a password. Some of you are probably thinking, "Our vendors"—I'm not going to name names, but you know who they are— "don't do that right now." If that's the case, ask for it. If a bunch of us are asking for this capability, it will start showing up in the vendors' product road maps.

Now that we have covered the events you should be auditing, it is time to set up alerts for those events. One alert should be for failed log-in attempts. If you have maybe five failed log-in attempts in a day, that should be enough to trigger an alert. And if somebody runs a script company-wide, I'd want to see an alert for this type of activity, too. Next, you will want to have alerts for after hour login events.

Some of you are hosting your own RMM on premises, or your solution is sitting inside of either your Office or a cloud you support. Maybe it's a data center or Azure. It doesn't matter where. If you have administrative access to the server itself, you should have the following things in place.

First, make sure your RMM server is living on its own VLAN—that it's not on the same VLAN as your workstations or your other servers or your domain controller. It's off in its own little space by itself. Speaking of domain controllers, do not join your RMM server to your active directory. If an attacker gets to your domain, you do not want them to be able to access your RMM. Set it up either on its own domain or make sure it's not on your domain at all. Why is this? Most MSPs we audit have a hard time locking down their active directory permissions. If attackers were to get into their domains, they would easily get access to the domain joined RMM.

Okay, but why put the RMM server on its own VLAN? It's time to talk SQL. You see, SQL is a legacy service: that is, I can log in to SQL without multifactor authentication. If you have your SQL ports open, you're going to run into a situation where somebody can bypass the multifactor authentication you set up by accessing the SQL back end of your RMM directly.

Be very careful. If you don't have the time to set up a VLAN for your RMM server at the moment, don't wait. At least set up the Windows Firewall to block SQL access.

Many RMMs create daily backups of their SQL databases locally, which is a good idea. You will want to make sure the jobs that are running these local backups are creating encrypted SQL backup files. Why do you want that? If attackers land on that server—let's say they launch a lateral attack and somehow get over to it—they can restore the SQL backup and get information they would need to use SQL injection or remotely access the devices you support.

Now let's talk about patching. Make sure you are applying the patches from the RMM vendor. You will also need to apply updates for SQL Server. Another area you will need to patch is the web server hosting your RMM. This could be IIS or maybe Apache. These patches don't necessarily come with your RMM updates.

Operating system updates are important as well. We audited an MSP in 2020 whose RMM was running out of Windows Server 2008. It wasn't even R2!

Okay, we covered some steps if you are hosting your own RMM. Here are a couple of areas you will want to address either way: self-hosted or cloud hosted. First, limit the number of IP addresses that have access to the console. You'll want the agents running on the computers you support to be able to check in from wherever they are. You've got a computer you support in Australia, you want that computer to be able to check in, but you don't want anybody to be able to log in to your RMM console from Australia. Limit the access to the console to your teams IP addresses. You could do that by allowing all IP addresses in the United States. I would suggest limiting RMM console access to trusted addresses—those in your office and employees' homes.

Keep track of your API keys. Check this list of keys often. Remember: API keys are like passwords. You want to keep them inside a password vault. Don't put them in a text file. These are the keys to the kingdom and a way to bypass multifactor authentication. Also, regularly review all the services that access them. Make sure they should still be around. When's the last time you looked through all the API keys you have published and made sure you don't have services that can access your RMM? Now would be a good time to check this out. I recommend auditing API keys at the same time you are auditing your multifactor account configurations.

Let's talk about the agents that check in and get commands from your RMM. First, you want the agents configured in such a way that if DNS goes down, the agents still check back in with you. That means you have a DNS address and an IP address for your RMM that the agent checks, and so if the DNS is missed for some reason, it'll still check in by IP.

Also, agents have a key built into them, a private key they use to prove to the RMMs that they're legitimate. Those keys were set when you first set up your RMM, especially some of the legacy RMMs out there, the ones that have been around for a long time.

Those keys were set as a default key. And if you haven't modified yours, that will create a problem down the road. So make sure your agent keys are not default keys. They should be randomly generated. Some vendors have a way to do this. If you're worried about it, submit a ticket and talk to the vendor about it.

Okay, we've covered everything you need to know about RMM security. One last point: don't put your RMM agents on your backup servers. If hackers get to your RMM, they will deploy ransomware through the scripting interface on all the machines inside the RMM. This would probably take around fifteen minutes. If they're able to do that to your backup servers too, you have data loss. Big time data loss for all of your clients at once. This is why I recommend you make sure your backup infrastructure does not have your RMM agents on it.

Some of you are probably wondering how to manage patching remotely. My recommendation is to either use the backup vendor's remote capabilities or run separate RMMs.

Last but not least, make sure your agents are getting updates from your server. You can check this just by checking the agent version, maybe even on your own computer. We've seen a number of cases in which the updates are working on the server but not getting out to the individual agents. Those agents are getting older, and you know where that leads: vulnerabilities and outages.

Let's talk about the steps you need to take to ensure you don't leave a gaping hole an attacker can drive a bus through.

First, create a script folder. Some MSPs put scripts all over the place on the devices they support. Don't be one of them.

If you create a script folder—let's say it's "system drive//galactic" —you can look there if there's something weird going on, maybe to see if somebody dropped a script you weren't expecting.

You also should whitelist scripts, especially if you're using some sort of zero-trust tool. But you don't want to whitelist the entire script folder. Let me repeat: don't whitelist the entire script folder. If you do, an attacker will know you have a script folder, because if he lands on an endpoint, he'll see it. He'll also guess that everything in there is whitelisted. Just whitelist the individual scripts.

Also, whitelist scripts based on their hashes. A lot of tools support hash-based whitelisting. But if you update your script, you have to update the hashes that go along with it.

In addition, don't embed API keys or passwords in the scripts themselves. Remember, these scripts are pushed out to the workstation, so if a hacker enumerates a workstation looking for passwords, looking for keys, that gives him the ability to use that API key to gain access to your password vault.

If you're interested in an RMM-hardening checklist, visit **GalacticScan.com/RMM-Checklist**.

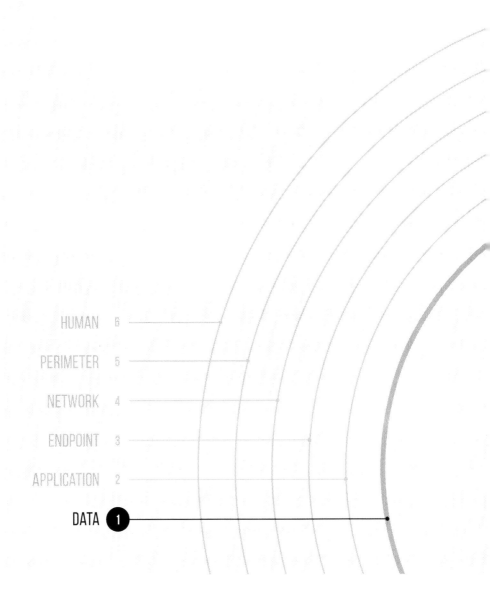

HUMAN 6

PERIMETER 5

NETWORK 4

ENDPOINT 3

APPLICATION 2

DATA 1

DATA

Data—in whatever form it takes—is the reason cybersecurity exists. It's the common denominator of all cybersecurity plans. Keeping your personally identifiable information safe, having functioning, ransomware-proof backups, and establishing a solid disaster recovery plan are all critical for you and your clients.

CHAPTER 17
PERSONALLY IDENTIFIABLE INFORMATION

In this chapter, I'm going to talk about the innermost ring of your security stack—your data.

And the data most important to you is your personally identifiable information. This includes things like your Social Security number, your date of birth, your first and last names, your address, and your mother's maiden name.

When I was running my MSP, I received a call one mid-February afternoon. I was sitting at my desk, and I picked up the phone. At the time, we had a receptionist. She rings me and says, "Hey, I have somebody from an accounting firm who wants to talk to you. He'd like us to do an audit for them."

And I thought, "What accountant in his right mind would want a security audit in February?" Because you know what happens in April, just two months from February. Taxes are due. Usually, accountants are tied up until the first week of May. I've never marketed to accounting firms during their busy season because I knew they weren't going to pop their heads up for air until after they've finished with putting together taxes. They only thing that happens between January and April in accounting firms is updates to their systems for tax changes. That's it. I knew something was up, so I took the call.

It seemed the caller wanted a credentialed audit. I asked why he wanted it in the middle of February. He hesitated for a few seconds. Finally, he explained that his firm was no longer able to do e-filing with the IRS.

Think about that. How do you file your taxes? Unless you live in a cave, you use e-filing. That's how most everybody in the world does it today. Can you imagine if your accountant said he couldn't do e-filing?

Obviously, this firm was screwed if they weren't able to even process an electronic tax return for one of their clients. I kept pushing. I asked why he needed a credentialed security audit in order to e-file. Then it all came out. Apparently, the IRS wouldn't allow the firm to e-file until it could provide a credentialed audit to prove that it was secure.

So we did the audit, and we did the forensic work and we discovered that an attacker had gotten access to one of its users' Microsoft 365 accounts. The user didn't email any PII, which is a real big no-no. (Just a reminder: never email PII, credit card numbers, or anything that's private.) Microsoft 365 didn't give the hacker access to any of that stuff.

Once the attacker got in, he noticed an email that came through from the user's online tax accounting software. He figured out that the firm was using a product for doing the taxes and filing returns. So he jumped over to this cloud hosted application and entered the user's email address to log in, then clicked the little button that said "forgot password."

Guess what happens when you forget your password? (Or guess what used to happen with this product in 2017?) It sent an email to you and allowed you to click on the email to change your password. At that point, the attacker changed the password, logged in, did a bunch of work, then logged off. When the user came in the next day, her password didn't work, so she reset it and went back to work.

This happened for four consecutive nights.

As a result, the hacker was able to e-file over 150 fraudulent tax returns for the accountant's clients. As he worked, he updated each filer's bank account routing information. So instead of the refund going to the person who should have gotten it, it went to the attacker. In the end, we found that this accounting firm had around 180 of these fraudulently filed returns by the time our audit was complete. This is exactly how much damage Microsoft 365 phishing attack can do. In fact, according to the IRS, there were $10.9 billion worth of fraudulent tax refunds claimed in 2015 alone.

Why is this such a big deal? Because once your identity is stolen, it's nearly impossible to submit your taxes to the IRS. The agency doesn't trust that your return came from you and not someone else. So you have to figure out a way to prove that you are who you say you are. By the way, as of April 2021 you can get a PIN from the IRS to allow you to keep someone from filing a tax return on your behalf.

Back to the issue, this is why protecting personally identifiable information is so important. If you lose it, it's really hard to recover it. After you've screwed around for three months trying to get your tax return to go through, you'll wish you didn't have the data breach in the first place. What data is most important to your business clients? Answer: it's their own clients' or patients' personally identifiable information. The next thing on the list is their employees' personally identifiable information. These are both very important to your clients because their reputation is on the line for these two items.

In one instance, an human resources person responded to a phishing email supposedly from her firm's CEO. The email said, "I need a copy of all W-2s ASAP. Here's my personal email address; I think my work email has been hacked." So, breaching employee confidentiality, she sent them over to that email address. I'm sure you can predict what happened. All those employees became victims of identity theft within six weeks of the phishing event.

Next up, your clients also want to protect their intellectual property—things like source code and processes and procedures that are proprietary to their organizations. They may not tell you they're worried about it, but deep down, they value it highly, especially if it's held for ransom.

Finally, we have accounting data. This can be things like receivables—money people owe them. It could even be contracts with other vendors, or a client database. These are all digital assets that can be classified as data.

Ransomware isn't just about forcing people to pay to recover their data anymore. Many hackers also threaten to post the data on the internet. This is called doxing. Imagine if one of your clients was breached, and the attacker said, "You need to send me 42.5 bitcoin in order to recover the data." (That's around $2.4 million, at the time of writing this book.) "If you don't send me the 42.5 bitcoin, I'm going to post your employees' and your clients' personal information on the web." That means putting it on a social channel like Twitter or Facebook, where anyone could find it. How would your client react? What would this do to their reputation?

Now, if you're supporting a hospital or a clinic, or anyone in the health-care industry, that's a disaster. Some of you outside the

United States don't have to deal with HIPAA, but it's still really painful when a hacker posts information about your clients or patients online. It's extremely difficult to recover from the loss of trust that comes with having all your data revealed on the internet. How does a doctor rebuild that trust with their patient?

What's the most important data for an MSP?

First, there's client data and all the backups of your client data is at the top of the list. I'm not just talking about backups here; I'm also thinking about the original data—the data that resides on their systems. Even if you can recover from a ransomware attack, even if you can keep a breach from happening, you'll still have, in many cases, a few days of downtime. That's an outage that lasts days for the client. Think about how that feels for your client and the amount of hours you will have to put in to recover their systems. I've never seen a ransomware attack that's taken less than 35 hours of engineering to clean up.

There's also your employees' personal data, and all the configuration information you hold inside your tools. The keys and passwords you use to access and support your client environments. And the digital certificates used to secure your website and other tools. You also have your business data like receivables and accounting reports. Not to mention your CRM data and your website. MSPs have a lot of data that is very important to them.

How do you protect this data? Let's start with backups.

Many of you use document management systems to hold all the configuration information for your clients. With most of these document management systems you can export your client configuration data into a runbook. On one occasion when I was performing a security analysis, I discovered a folder full of runbooks. These were PDFs that included all the client's configuration information, all its passwords for every single device on its network. Basically, the folder contained everything about how that client's network was set up and how to access it.

This could be a really handy disaster recovery mechanism.

It might even be part of your disaster recovery plan.
As in, back up these runbooks once every month.

But *where* you back them up is critical. The runbooks I discovered were sitting in a folder that was shared through OneDrive for everybody in the organization to see.

Think like a hacker for a minute. What would you do if you could lay your hands on all the passwords and network topography, including the backups, for a hundred businesses? I bet you could come up with some options.

So how do you currently deal with holding and backing up this type of sensitive information?

Most managed service providers today figure, "Okay, we'll have our tools take care of it." But think about those runbooks for a second. Why did they end up on OneDrive? Because the person who exported them was told to export them all as part of the disaster recovery processes. I've seen other MSPs export runbooks in order to do a client handoff.

What this really comes down to is: you've got to get people to think about confidential information and how to keep it confidential. You have to think about protecting your data. You have to think about protecting your clients' data, and their clients' data, and so on. You also have to think about your tools and what they're doing. How do you protect the data in those tools?

Assume attackers can access everything on your computer:
What could they get? Because at some point, somebody will get through your layers of security.

One way to prevent this is to limit access through encryption.

How many of you encrypt all the computers in your network with BitLocker? BitLocker offers full-drive encryption. That helps when attackers harvest data they've gotten physical access to.

Maybe somebody stole a computer, or you made a mistake and didn't destroy one of the drives for a client you support. Maybe a hypervisor got breached. These are all situations in which a hacker can gain physical access to a device. This type of event is protected by the type of full drive encryption provided by BitLocker.

What if the hacker gets into the network you support? If he does, he's likely going to go through the layers of your defense using phishing. He will probably move laterally across the network using methods like pass the hash. He'll have access to the unencrypted drive because you've entered your credentials. This means he'll have access to the files inside the encrypted drive even when you use full-drive encryption. One of the biggest issues with data protection through encryption is that the data has to be decrypted for the user to access it. When an attacker phishes their way in, they gain access to this data.

What about cloud storage? What if you upload something onto OneDrive and Microsoft loses one of its keys? OneDrive is a wonderful security solution, and it has great encryption. But it's only awesome until it loses a key. The same goes for Dropbox and other file-sharing tools. And what about those files you downloaded, like your taxes? How do you deal with them?

One question I often hear is: "Why don't we just use the encryption built into PDFs, Word files, and Excel files?"

Here's the issue. Those are all pretty easy to bypass, and if you don't believe me, I've gotten more than five million results by bypassing encryption on a PDF file. In some instances, it costs money, somewhere around $12, or maybe $50 for a tool, to bypass encryption. But do you think an attacker wouldn't spend $50 on a PDF ripper if he could use it to gain access to a thousand PDFs? Think about a small medical clinic you support. What if its PDFs contained billing information? And all it cost was $50 for a simple tool to get inside them?

To protect yourself, you can use an encrypted vault. Basically, you create a small drive, and you store that drive on your Dropbox, or on your OneDrive, and then you encrypt it.

You use a key, a long password, to get into it. There's a little tool that's super easy to use called VeraCrypt. It creates a file and allows you to mount it as a drive on your computer. This is a good way to protect data that you don't want an attacker to access.

I can hear it now. I can hear somebody typing an email to let me know that he uses BitLocker for this. But here's the thing: you can create a BitLocker VHD or VHDX file, but you have to have local admin rights in order to dismount. You have to have access to the drive tool inside Windows in order to manage what's mounted and what's not mounted. You'll end up having to give your users local admin rights. We all know that's a bad thing, because local admins have other rights, too, one of those being the ability to get to everything on the computer. This means if that user gets phished the attacker can easily move laterally across the network.

Set up your VeraCrypt, create an encrypted file that you can mount as a drive and you are off to the races. If you choose to store the file on cloud storage, I suggest you keep the file under 600 MB in size. The reason for this is that if you make the file as big as a gig, it's going to take a really long time to sync up. And the way to avoid differences in your file over time—syncing differences between your cloud storage and your local machine—is keeping that file size small. Create a strong key for the password on the file and store that in your password manager. Only mount it when you need access to the confidential data you store on it, and when you're not using it, dismount it, because then an attacker can't get to you without your password.

One caveat: there's no way to recover this password. If you forget it or lose it, you're screwed. Your backup won't save you, because your backup is an encrypted file.

Alright, now that you have a way to store your confidential information, there's one more thing we need to discuss. In 2018, one of my clients took screenshots of a number of errors that were popping up when she was scanning patient data for a small medical clinic. She created ten screenshots of that data.

She was responsible for billing, and that data contained all sorts of personal health information about each of her patients. You can imagine all of the stuff that has to go into a patient record in order to get the clinic's insurance provider to pay for the visit.

Those screenshots were then uploaded into our RMM, and they ended up in the ticket. If someone takes a screenshot of patient information, *bam*—your RMM is storing personally identifiable information. This is even worse, because it is personally identifiable information for a medical practice, which means now the RMM we are running contains personal health information.

This is what I call compliance creep. If we leave that data in the RMM it is now covered by HIPAA and it now contains a considerable amount of sensitive information. How do you stop this sort of thing? How do you keep this from happening?

First, tell your clients never to take a picture of a screen that includes personally identifiable information. If your engineer finds it, establish a protocol to remove it. Maybe your engineer shouldn't be able to delete screenshots or delete tickets or remove data from backups, but somebody on your team should have that ability. Think back to the different types of users I had you create inside your RMM. This might be something you want a user with administrative permissions to take care of.

Your mission for this chapter is to outline your protocol for moving personally identifiable information and other confidential information if it gets into your RMM. This mission should take you no more than twenty minutes.

CHAPTER 18
BACKUPS

The first time I got involved with paying a ransom and helping a client get its data back was in mid-October of 2017.

There was a law firm who was hit with ransomware, and its MSP was backing up data on tape drives. The MSP required the firm to swap the drives every day, and there was a system set up so that if there was a failure, the MSP would get an alert.

The problem was that the backup job got hung up around March. The backups never really failed—they just didn't complete. So if you're alerting on failure only, and you never look to see whether there has been a success, then you'll never know if you have a backup job hung up preventing further backups from happening.

When the law firm contacted us, they had been down for around four days. The firm was trying to get its MSP to recover the data. Obviously, with no backup job running there had been no backup data since March.

Can you imagine being that MSP and trying to explain to your client that even though you're getting paid for managing backups, and even though these backup tapes are being swapped out of the server daily, you haven't completed a good backup in six months? Just think about the amount of work that thirty-five attorneys would lose in six months' time.

The only thing we could do in this case was to pay the ransom and rebuild everything.

Anatomy of a Ransom

For those of you who haven't ever paid a ransom, here's how it starts. First, you need to purchase bitcoin. In this case, it cost only around $40,000, so it wasn't super expensive. We see ransoms a lot higher than that today, but it was expensive enough. You could buy a new car for $40,000 in cash.

The next thing you need to do is contact the hacker over a Tor network connection. He'll usually have a site somewhere on the dark web with a URL that ends in .onion. Sometimes you have to test a couple of files to make sure the encryption keys work. It all depends on the situation, and who you are dealing with on the other end.

Then you send the bitcoin, and you wait. You just sent $40,000 in untraceable nonrefundable bitcoin to someone who claims they can unlock your data to get your business going again. In our case, it took around thirty-six hours for the hacker to get back to us. Just imagine the stress you're under for thirty-six hours before you receive a response.

When the hacker gets back to you, he sends you a link to an application, and he sends you a code. Basically, you have to run this application and insert the code. Then the application slowly decrypts the files, one by one—it goes through and recovers your data. In our case, when we were around two gigs into the recovery, the application stopped. We had to get a new code and start again. This happened to us multiple times. Even hackers have bugs.

At this point, a couple of alarm bells should be going off in your head. First, you've identified yourself as somebody willing to pay a ransom for your data. You're also forced to run an application that a hacker provided on your network, and that application won't work unless it's connected to the internet.

If you ever get into this situation, know that it's not a fast process. It takes a very long time to recover from ransomware, probably much longer than it takes to restore data from that tape drive. One quick suggestion, if you are going through this type of recovery process, you should install a UTM device between the machine you're recovering and the outside world. If you contact me or someone on my staff, we'd be happy to go through all this stuff with you. The reason you insert a UTM device is because the application the hacker gave you could harvest data and push it outside the network while it's recovering the files. You wouldn't know about it unless you had some tools in place to see it.

The other thing you want to do is reformat everything on your network and rebuild, because the hacker had admin rights to the environment. Remember, if the client has regulatory pressure or a documented incident response plan, follow it. You may have to preserve evidence.

You can see that this becomes a very, very expensive big deal very quickly.

How do you keep an attacker from making it in in the first place? Well, the answer is really simple: a good security stack and a great backup strategy. In this chapter we are focused on the backup strategy.

Backup Strategy

Always start formulating your backup strategy by asking a very easy question: What are you backing up? Which data is important in your organization? If you're a typical MSP, one thing you probably have is a PSA. A PSA is responsible for storing tickets and client information. It keeps track of all your client data, contracts, tickets, and all that other jazz you need to support your clients. The other thing you probably have is an accounting system, some sort of general ledger, maybe QuickBooks. We see a lot of QuickBooks files and human resources-related documents on public shares within MSP networks. These are things like I-9s and W-2s and all the confidential information you store about your team. Then you have your file system, which contains things like Excel and Word documents, and then you have your RMM, responsible for running scripts, keeping track of configurations, and alerting. Those are the typical tools we see inside an MSP. And each one has a different recovery time objective.

Now that we have put together a list of the assets you will want to make sure that you are actually backing them up. The next element of your strategy is your recovery point objective (RPO)—that is, the point in time from which your data needs to be restored. For example, do you want to restore data from as recently (or as far back) as yesterday? If you have an event today at ten o'clock at night, is it okay to restore back from data that was from last week? Or do you need to restore to the last hour? The shorter the recovery point objective—i.e., the shorter the amount of time between the event and your objective—the less data you will lose when you get back up and running.

Let's consider some recovery point objectives for your various business tools. First, the PSA. I recommend a one-hour recovery point objective.

You've got tickets flowing in. If you lose them for a day, that can be a real challenge. You want your clients to understand that you have their backs if you lose more than, let's say, a few minutes of ticket history. But I realize that some of you have PSAs combined with other tools. So if you put your tickets in the same place as your automation, for example, you'll want to push your automation recovery point objective to hourly as well.

For accounting software and human resources data, you might want to set your recovery point objective to be one day. There's not a lot of change in accounting data for MSPs. With such little change in the dataset, you could probably even go to a full week of recovery point objective, but I don't recommend it.

Okay, now that we have a couple of recovery point objectives defined, another part of your strategy is your recovery time objective, or RTO —basically, how long will it take to restore everything. Ask yourself how long your business can go without each particular tool before there's a problem or a gap in your business continuity planning. This will become your recovery time objective. With most MSPs, I recommend a 4-hour recovery time objective. When you push it down smaller than four hours, the costs become over burdensome.

Backup Methods

Now let's look at the various types of backup methods you can choose from.

One is nearline storage, or nearline backups. These are devices, perhaps servers, that are usually located in the same building as your business. They're used for backups performed daily, hourly, or sometimes every few minutes.

Another type is off-site backups. These are usually cloud solutions. Backups can either be taken directly to these off-site backups, or the nearline backups can push the backup data to them.

Next we have offline backups. You're probably wondering what the difference is between off-site and offline backups. Offline backups involve off-site storage that's not available after the backups are created. Glacier can be one example. You have a key that's generated once, and you can never get to your data again without that key. It's considered offline because you're not writing to it again, ever.

Next we have physical backups. Those are drives such as tape drives and hard drives that get physically swapped out. You want your drive to be air gapped—disconnected completely from the network—before it's swapped. Of course, these require a lot more effort on your part because you have to swap the drives all the time.

Finally, we have long-term backups, or archival backups, which are usually in place to assist with regulatory compliance or to prevent employee espionage or damage. These backups are usually performed every ninety days, every six months, or maybe even just annually, after you close out your books and tie everything up.

Archival backups are important because sometimes it takes a while to realize that something bad happened to your data. Let's say you fire a team member, and before he leaves he deletes a bunch of files. And you don't notice for a couple of months. Archival backups allow that type of data to be recovered.

Keep in mind that all these types of backups—nearline, off-site, offline, physical, and archival—are not to be confused with redundancy. I'm sure at least one or two readers are thinking, "We have a mirror—we have servers working in duplicate"

The difference between redundancy and backups is that redundancy involves writing data to two different drives or two different servers in very close to real time. There's no way to go back through your history. Backups allow you to recover files and/or entire systems written over a specific period of time. Think about redundancy, like having dual tires on a truck. I know you've seen those when you are sitting behind a semi. Backups would be more like the spare tire in your trunk. If you run over a huge pothole with the dual tires, they would both get damaged. (I'm talking a New Orleans size pothole here, google it.) The spare tire, on the other hand would be undamaged.

Backup Security

Back in 2019, I was auditing a hospital that had around one hundred beds and 1,800 employees. To back up their data, they used an image-based backup product. It had the ability to back up Exchange and SQL and several other tools they were running.

The hospital was having some trouble with backups completing, so one of the support team members made the share public and allowed Everyone to write to it. This is one of the things we often see when it comes to backups and troubleshooting. When people have problems, they start changing permissions. The hospital basically changed the permissions and made the share public, so that anybody on the network could get to it. I know, you are thinking to yourself, this story is going to end in ransomware attacking that publicly shared backup drive. Read on.

The hospital also missed a step with configuration. You see, they didn't encrypt the backups. That meant that anybody who downloaded a trial of Acronis could restore those backups without a password or any other kind of effort. The hospital had its permissions set up right on the servers. The users were set up only to be able to access the data they needed to do their jobs. But if you just went to the backups, you could bypass that and get access to all the hospital's patient information as well as all of its employee information.

So as you can see, even big organizations get this wrong. This screw-up is by no means confined to MSPs.

What can you learn from this? First, make sure you encrypt your backup data. That's how things work in the twenty-first century. If you don't encrypt everything, and somebody troubleshoots—or maybe over-troubleshoots—something, like a share, you can have a data leak on your hands. And we all want to avoid that. If you have backups that aren't encrypted—maybe those created with Robocopy—Consider putting them into an encrypted container rather than writing them directly to their destination.

In backup land, I like to think you should have three lives. You have your original best set of data, a nearline backup, and offline storage of some sort. Make sure you always have three types. Then, if an attacker is able to access the nearline backups but can't get to the offsite backups, you are safe. But if they get to all of them, that's when you have to pay a ransom. How do you keep them from getting to all three of your data sets?

There are a few things I'd like to bring up here. The first one is: the file systems that contain your backups should not be available to the rest of the network. Don't let your backup software write to SMB shares, for example. We've seen attackers use registry entries from backup software to find where the backups go and destroy them.

Also, never, ever, ever cache backup credentials. We see this often when engineers connect to backup devices from servers within the network the backups are protecting. Warn your team and provide them training on avoiding this behavior. Never, ever log in to a server that's being backed up and then go from that server to the backup device to do a restore of a file.

Do you not manage backup devices from inside the client network?

If you try to save yourself time by installing your RMM agents on your backup devices so you can manage their patches and other things through your RMM, you might want to think again. Because that means that if an attacker does get to your RMM, he can also get to your backups. Sometimes that means he is getting to all three sets of your backups. So if he uses your RMM to push out ransomware to all your clients, he could also destroy your backups in the process. It's a good idea not to manage your backups from inside your RMM.

Don't have RMM agents installed on your backup infrastructure, and don't store passwords inside the RMM for your backup or your backup servers. All these things give an attacker access to your backup data and your client's original data. And obviously, never leave your backups mounted on one of your client's computers, because if it's mounted, the path can be followed by an attacker.

I want you to think like an attacker when you're thinking about your backups, and I want you to make sure that nobody gets to that very critical piece of infrastructure inside your organization.

Backup Testing

There are a lot of backup devices and backup solutions out there. When it comes to testing them, a lot of these solutions have the ability to boot up a virtual machine in order to validate that the backup is working.

Let me ask you this: How many of you are using backups and testing them by just booting up a virtual machine? You boot it up, you look at the login page, or maybe your backup software automatically boots up the virtual machine and takes a screenshot for you. Maybe it even puts a screenshot in a ticket for you so you can close it out and be done with it.

Let me ask you another question: Do you use more than one drive on your servers? Perhaps a C drive for an operating system and a D drive for data? Maybe you use data and a logs drive in a transaction drive for your SQL Servers?

If we were sitting in a room together, I think everybody's hand would go up, because breaking up data and operating systems is a standard method for setting up and creating your server infrastructure.

Would it still boot up if the data drive wasn't mounted? Would a VM still boot up if you could just get to the C drive and the data drive wasn't mounted?

Heck, yeah, it would. It's a little dangerous to test your backups just by making sure the virtual copies of your servers boot up, if the data drives don't come up with them, you'd never know. If you have a C and D drive, for example, and the D drive was corrupted, this server boot test you are doing would not detect it.

So how should you test?

The first thing, obviously, is to boot the virtual machine, just like you are doing now. The other piece, though, is to restore a file. Restore a file from each of the critical drives on the system.

Here is a spot where you can use some automation to speed things up. We do it by creating a file in a folder that contains some critical information. Then we change something about that file every day. You can do that really simply by putting a date in the file and then MD5 hashing it. So that way you know you're always changing more than just a date—you're changing the bits of an MD5 hash.

Then you wait. After a period of time, you request a file, or you restore a file from the historically seeded drive. For example, you might go back five days or ten days and restore a file from your data drive. That will prove to you that the data drive is not only mountable but also has viable data on it. You can do this inside your RMM with a little bit of scripting.

Okay, now that we have testing out of the way, and you know you have viable backups, what else should you do to protect them? If you integrate your backups to Active Directory, and an attacker is capable of getting to Active Directory, he will then be able to either damage or destroy your backups. Do not integrate your backups with Active Directory. Create a separate network for all your backups.

Finally, many backup solutions out there have multifactor authentication capabilities built in. Make sure you enable them. But be very, very careful, because even if you have multifactor authentication set up to manage the front end of the backups, attackers can get around to the back end using the SMB shares and other things you created by integrating with Active Directory—yet another reason not to integrate your backups with Active Directory. And remember that service accounts usually bypass multifactor authentication.

As you're putting together your backup strategy, whether for your organization or for your clients, make sure to incorporate the right pieces, be they redundancy with mirroring; some sort of nearline backup, so you can restore stuff quickly; an offline solution, air gapped to prevent backups from being accessible to the internal network; and some sort of archiving solution, especially if your clients are under regulatory pressure. Also, be careful about where you store your credentials and how you get from your management tools to your backups.

CHAPTER 19
DISASTER RECOVERY

Alright, you made it. We are on the last chapter.
Now, I want to talk about the worst thing you can do
if you're working at or running an MSP.

I mean the absolute worst thing possible. I'm talking about the thing that destroys the trust that you spent years earning. Something that makes your users stop trusting you. Something that makes your employees stop trusting you. Something that makes the leadership in the organizations you support lose faith in you.

I'm talking about the ultimate sin when it comes to IT: data loss.

If your organization or one of your clients experiences data loss on your watch, you will never regain that trust. You will never be able to build that trust back up to the level you enjoyed before the data loss occurred.

Your clients may act like they trust you, but they'll always have this little voice in the back of their heads, wondering, "Do I really trust that the engineers at my MSP are doing what they say they're doing? They couldn't even get our backups right."

Ultimately, you want your clients to think you're a hero. To achieve that, you need to get very, very clear about their expectations when it comes to backup and disaster recovery.

So, the following are the best practices you want to put in place.

Disaster Recovery Fundamentals

The most important thing you must do—and I talk about this over and over and over—is encrypt the data that's at rest while you're backing it up. By this I mean using a commercially sound encryption solution, not just obfuscation or some sort of hashing.

I list this first because if you don't do it right out of the gate, it's hard to fix. Imagine having to go back and reconfigure all your backups to set up encryption. In that case you would have weeks or months or years of data that's not encrypted. You have to decide: Do I destroy all that data? Or do I go back through and encrypt that data manually?

You also need to use distinct keys or distinct passwords during the process of encryption for each of your servers. If you're using passwords, they should be generated by a machine, not by a user —you shouldn't be sitting there typing letters on a keyboard. You also want passwords that are around twenty characters, or longer if your tools can support it.

In addition, you need to protect your keys and passwords, which means storing them in a place you can access if you experience your own disaster. If your keys are stored in a spot that you can get to right now but that wouldn't be accessible if the event that affected the customer also affected your organization, you'd have a problem on your hands. Store those keys in an encrypted vault or on an encrypted drive, and consider creating multiple copies of them.

One thing about encrypted vaults and encrypted drives: never mount them unless you're trying to access the data held inside them. This is especially important in relation to backup keys.

The other thing I see out in the field pretty often is that MSPs aren't updating their backup systems. Your backup vendor releases patches, just as your operating-system vendor does, and you need to download and install them. If you don't, the encryption you're planning to use might not work the way you expect. Your restore might not work the way you expect. There might be a security flaw in the backup that could allow an attacker into the system. An attacker might use the backup engine or scheduler itself against you. Sign up for emails about patches and security alerts from your backup vendor and apply those patches.

Finally, you need to set up an alert to let you know when a backup is not successful. But an alert that goes off only when a backup isn't successful is not sufficient. You should also create an alert for backups that *are* successful as well as for those that are incomplete (see page 187 for a case in point). And the system should check for this alert on a daily basis.

RPO, RTO, and MAO

When you're planning your clients' disaster recovery protocol, several questions will crop up, such as, "How long should I hold on to backup data?" "Where should I store backup data?" "Should I back up the data every day? Or every week?" "Should I push backup data off-site every day? Every month? Or every hour?"

In order to answer those questions, you need to have a discussion about backups with your clients. Ask them which of their data would be hardest to replace in the event of a loss. Maybe it's data that would take hours to reproduce, or maybe it's data that's impossible to reproduce, such as the results of a series of tests on a patient or product.

Once you identify that data, then you can ask where it's stored. Then you can ask how long your clients can go without it.

Let's say a client had a fire. Would it be okay to lose one day's worth of data? Five days' worth of data? Ten days' worth of data? Or maybe it's only okay to lose ten minutes of data.

Also, if it takes you twenty-four hours to recover twelve hours' worth of lost data, your client will end up losing thirty-six hours' worth of data between the data that was lost and the twenty-four hours of recovery time.

This is where RPO (recovery point objective), RTO (recovery time objective), and MAO (maximum acceptable outage) come in.

Imagine that the thick black line in the diagram below represents time.

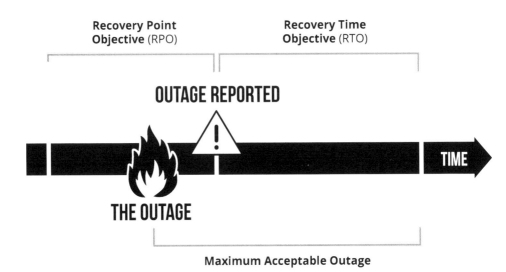

Maximum Acceptable Outage

Then imagine that your client has an event. Maybe a server disintegrates. **This white triangle represents the point when your client lets you know that the server is gone**, or maybe it represents the point when an alert pops up and lets you know that the server went offline. **The flame represents the outage itself**.

You know that a backup occurred at some point before the server disappeared and before you were alerted to it. The amount of time between that backup and the disaster itself is the amount of time it's acceptable for each particular data asset to lose. That's where you set your recovery point objective, or RPO.

The RTO, or recovery time objective, is the amount of time it will take from the point when you found out about the disaster to the point when everything will come back online. That's what you communicate to your client in advance: "It will take me three days, Mr. Client," or "It will take me three hours, Ms. CEO, to get you back online."

There's one other number you want to establish, which is the maximum acceptable outage, or MAO. You set that number on your alerts: how quickly do they have to tell you when an event happens? An hour afterward? Three minutes afterward?

You should keep a record of each one of these three things —RPO, RTO, and MAO—for all your clients, not just for their environments but also for their critical data. You might be thinking, "Holy cow, that's a problem. How am I going to keep track of all that?"

After you have that all documented, it's time to create a testing strategy—that is, a way to test your ability to reach your RPO. Measure the time between the outage and the most recent backup as well as the time between the outage and the restoration, and make sure they're acceptable to your clients.

LEVELING UP

This isn't the end, it is just the beginning.
You are on a journey. We are all on a journey as we improve the security and controls in our businesses.

I've shared some of the findings, battle stories, and lessons learned from the field and my own experiences running my MSP. I've given you steps that you can take to harden your own MSP, and ways you can protect your clients. It's time. You can do it. Get started with simple steps.

Here are a couple ideas of where to go from here:

Revisit Chapter 3 and get started on just-in-time documentation. This is the foundation for all of the other changes and improvements you will be making in your company.

Check out Chapter 13 and consider how you might improve your endpoint security. What steps could you take to make your endpoints hacker-proof? You've come this far, is it time to have a third party take a look at your stack?

Go over Chapter 15. Create an incident response plan. Make sure your entire team knows about it and is ready to use it. If you already have one, update it.

These are just a couple thoughts on where to start. People ask me all the time, "There's so much to do, where should I even start?"

It is simple, don't get overwhelmed. Don't hesitate.
The most important step you can take is the first one.
No matter what that is for you.

We have a long journey ahead of us. **I know you can do it**. I know you've got it in you. Just get started and create one improvement a week. Don't try to change everything, just small steps.

As you know, my goal is to help protect a million people.

Do me a favor, let me know how you are doing on your journey. Tell me about one thing you improved or one thing you found useful in this book. Tell me about something you are doing or did that you learned here. Go to www.galacticscan.com/levelup and share your win.

Tell me how you are making your MSP better. Tell me how you are creating a better more secure environment for yourself and your clients. Tell me how you are making your investment in security your competitive advantage. I can't wait to hear from you.

Most importantly: keep moving, improving, and helping our community become a better, safer place for our clients and our own businesses.

Dedicated to our community and your security,

—Bruce

ACKNOWLEDGEMENTS

I would like to thank all of those who go out of their way to help people. You are the ones who see someone struggling and reach out your hand. Thank you for making our world a better place.

Now for the people who helped me on this journey:

My partner Adam. He never lets me stop and be satisfied with my current iteration of success. To the infinity and beyond! (Stolen from a plastic toy, but it sums up our path forward.)

My mom and dad. They taught me the joy of helping others, and always believe in me.

Rita Poston. The lady that helps me keep my sh!t straight. Literally a full time job. Thanks Rita!

Robin Robins. She taught me how business gets done. She's a great person to have in your corner. Doesn't matter if it's a fight or a business deal.

Julie Hill. The woman whose been able to read my mind and create the designs / layouts / brands / art that represents my ideas.

Jeff Cameron. With his acute command of the English language.

Dave and Judi, Rocky and Sharon, Daphne and Fred, Nicole and Curt, Ron and Doug, Gerry and Troy, Kerry and Jo, and all my other partners in crime. The people who are constantly supporting my crazy ass ideas and watching me figure out the next big thing.

My partners and clients. The business owners who are leveling up their MSP businesses.

Level Up has more practical security advice in its 100+ pages than I have ever found in an IT security book.

Level Up is an informative field guide for MSPs and IT Security Professionals. It offers a straightforward roadmap to help you secure your environments. After all, getting started is the hardest part of any endeavor especially security. Bruce shares practical steps and wise advice to help you get started and make IT security management realistic and achievable. We've collaborated with Bruce and his teams since 2014 and his insights, practical advice and perspectives continue to help us keep security at the forefront of our business.

– Jennifer L. Holmes
Partner, MIS Solutions, Inc.

It is paramount that we (MSPs) get our own house in order, this book is the first step.

Level Up is an Awesome recipe book for MSPs to follow to help protect their most important assets. Bruce provides a powerful yet simple set of principles that are essential to combating threat actors. He has given us a great repeatable model to get us on track, hold us accountable and train us to ensure we are doing the right thing. He is a great resource, and the MSP community much better because of Bruce's efforts. Security is what keeps the owners of MSPs up at night. I cannot say I sleep like a baby but after implementing the items in this book, I do sleep better!!

– Corey Kirkendoll
CCIE/CCSA/CFS, President/CEO, 5K Technical Services

We are using the tips and tricks we've learned HERE to secure, grow, and scale our business.

Bruce's ability to break down the multifaceted concept of "security" into simple steps, that equate to obtainable goals, is unmatched in this industry. His approach is like the old adage, how do you eat an elephant? One bite at a time. He is brilliant and is not just giving lip service to ideas - he WAS an MSP and grew his business by using the same techniques he teaches, techniques that work!

– Brandis Kelly
Director of Operations, The Technology Specialist, Inc.

This book is a must for any IT security professional or MSP Company.

Having run a Security Focused MSP for over 25 years while also mentoring other MSPs for the last decade, I know the challenges IT Professionals face in securing networks and client's data. Level Up provides powerful, practical, and straightforward advice and systems for securing networks in today's world of ever-changing and evolving cyber threats. Security in the Managed Services business and IT in general has quickly become as important as cash flow – without it, your business will die. Everyone has a product, a service or a tactic but few are willing to share a complete strategy to help ensure your success. Bruce offers a comprehensive system in Level Up that is needed for IT Pros. If you are interested in leveling up your organization to ensure you can remain relevant in an increasingly security focused world, then this is a must read.

– Lliam W. Holmes
CCISO/CISSP/CCSP/CHFI/CISA/CISM, CEO MIS Solutions, Inc.

If you have an IT business with any responsibility for cyber security, stop what you are doing and read this book RIGHT NOW.

At the most critical time in history: businesses of all sizes and industries are under attack, Bruce has been an invaluable resource for companies like mine to help defend ourselves and harden our clients IT environments. Bruce is literally standing in the gap, a massive gap created by sophisticated nation state hackers that make no distinction on who they bring destruction to. I cannot imagine not having a resource like this to help my company and our security team navigate these rough waters. Because of Bruce, my company is running in high gear, making weekly security improvements and setting ourselves apart as leaders in cyber security.

– Neal Juern, President/CEO, Juern Technology

"Level Up" is an appropriate name for this book!

As MSPs we can no longer be 'computer fix-it' or 'server install' guys. We MUST 'level-up' our operations, procedures, documentation, philosophy and approach to our work and our Clients or be left in the dust of those of us who are. If you are looking for a playbook to start your journey or a guide along the way, you found it.

– Leia Shilobod, CEO/IT Princess of Power, InTech Solutions, Inc.